THE IMPORTANCE OF

Benjamin Franklin

by
Gail B. Stewart

Lucent Books, P.O. Box 289011, San Diego, CA 92198-9011

These and other titles are included in The Importance Of biography series:

Christopher Columbus
Marie Curie
Benjamin Franklin
Galileo Galilei
Chief Joseph
Richard M. Nixon
Jackie Robinson
H.G. Wells

Library of Congress Cataloging-in-Publication Data

Stewart, Gail B., 1949–
    Benjamin Franklin / by Gail B. Stewart.
        p.   cm. — (The Importance of)
    Includes bibliographical references and index.
    Summary: A biography of patriot Benjamin Franklin, from his Boston boyhood to his years as inventor and diplomat.
    ISBN 1-56006-026-3 (alk. paper)
    1. Franklin, Benjamin, 1706–1790—Juvenile literature.
    2. Statesman—United States—Biography—Juvenile literature.
    3. Scientists—United States—Biography—Juvenile literature.
    4. Printers—United States—Biography—Juvenile literature.
    [1. Franklin, Benjamin, 1706–1790.   2. Statesman.]   I. Title.
    II. Series.
    E302.6.F8S887   1992
    973.3'092–dc20
    [B]   92-23315
                                                              CIP
                                                               AC

Copyright 1992 by Lucent Books, Inc., P.O. Box 289011, San Diego, California, 92198-9011

Contents

Foreword

THE IMPORTANCE OF biography series deals with individuals who have made a unique contribution to history. The editors of the series have deliberately chosen to cast a wide net and include people from all fields of endeavor. Individuals from politics, music, art, literature, philosophy, science, sports, and religion are all represented. In addition, the editors did not restrict the series to individuals whose accomplishments have helped change the course of history. Of necessity, this criterion would have eliminated many whose contribution was great, though limited. Charles Darwin, for example, was responsible for radically altering the scientific view of the natural history of the world. His achievements continue to impact the study of science today. Others, such as Chief Joseph of the Nez Percé, played a pivotal role in the history of their own people. While Joseph's influence does not extend much beyond the Nez Percé, his nonviolent resistance to white expansion and his continuing role in protecting his tribe and his homeland remain an inspiration to all.

These biographies are more than factual chronicles. Each volume attempts to emphasize an individual's contributions both in his or her own time and for posterity. For example, the voyages of Christopher Columbus opened the way to European colonization of the New World. Unquestionably, his encounter with the New World brought monumental changes to both Europe and the Americas in his day. Today, however, the broader impact of Columbus's voyages is being critically scrutinized. *Christopher Columbus,* as well as every biography in The Importance Of series, includes and evaluates the most recent scholarship available on each subject.

Each author includes a wide variety of primary and secondary source quotations to document and substantiate his or her work. All quotes are footnoted to show readers exactly how and where biographers derive their information, as well as provide stepping stones to further research. These quotations enliven the text by giving readers eyewitness views of the life and times of each individual covered in The Importance Of series.

Finally, each volume is enhanced by photographs, bibliographies, chronologies, and comprehensive indexes. For both the casual reader and the student engaged in research, The Importance Of biographies will be a fascinating adventure into the lives of people who have helped shape humanity's past, present, and will continue to shape its future.

Important Dates in the Life of Benjamin Franklin

Born on January 17 in Boston —	**1706**	⌐ Apprenticed as a printer
		to his brother James
Silence Dogood essays published ⌐	**1718** ⌐	
anonymously in the *New England Courant* └	**1722**	⌐ Runs away from James and the print
		shop; sails to New York, then on to
	1723 ┘	Philadelphia
	1724–	
	1726	— Works as a printer in England
Forms the Junto —	**1727**	
Opens his own print shop —	**1728**	
	1730 ┘	⌐ Becomes owner of the *Pennsylvania*
		Gazette; marries Deborah Read
First edition of *Poor Richard's Almanack* —	**1732**	
	1736	— Becomes clerk of General Assembly
Becomes postmaster of Philadelphia —	**1737**	
	1741	— Designs Franklin stove
Founds American Philosophical Society —	**1743**	⌐ Writes first letters about his
	1747 ┘	experiments with electricity
Retires from business; elected ⌐		
as delegate to General Assembly └	**1748**	
	1752	— First lightning rod installed
Appointed deputy postmaster ⌐	**1753**	
general of North America └	**1754** ┘	⌐ Albany Congress delegate from
		Pennsylvania
Goes to London as agent for ⌐		
Pennsylvania └	**1757**	
Returns to Philadelphia —	**1762**	⌐ Massacre of native Americans
		by Paxton Boys; returns to London
	1764 ┘	as agent for Pennsylvania
	1765	— Stamp Act passes on February 27
Hutchinson letter scandal; ⌐	**1766**	— Stamp Act repealed
Franklin attacked before Britain's		
Privy Council; Deborah dies └	**1774**	
Returns to Philadelphia; —	**1775**	⌐ Helps formulate Declaration
elected to Continental Congress		of Independence; sails for
	1776	France to negotiate a treaty
	1778	— Treaty with France signed on February 6
British surrender; Franklin asked ⌐	**1781**	
to help negotiate peace settlement └		
	1785 ┘	⌐ Returns to Philadelphia;
		elected to Constitutional Convention
Constitution is written and accepted —	**1787**	
	1790	— Dies in Philadelphia on April 17

A Harmonious Human Multitude

The morning of April 21, 1790, was chilly and grey in Philadelphia. Gusts of wind were stripping bare many of the trees' early blooms. The unseasonable weather made it seem that winter would begin again.

Even with the unseasonably cold temperatures, a large crowd was beginning to gather at Independence Hall. Although the funeral procession would not begin for another two hours, people wanted to get there early. It was a historic day: Philadelphia was burying Benjamin Franklin.

No Surprise

When Franklin died on April 17, it should have been no surprise. After all, at a time when it was highly unusual for anyone to live to be seventy years old, Franklin had lived to be eighty-four. Besides, he had been bedridden and in pain for more than a year.

Nevertheless, when special issue number 3125 of the *Pennsylvania Gazette* appeared, with its striking black border and its large headlines announcing Franklin's death, the news was still a shock. Benjamin Franklin had been considered a fundamental part of the development of the young republic of America, and especially in his home city of Philadelphia. As one man wrote in his journal soon after

This portrait of the mature Ben Franklin painted by Joseph Duplessis is one of the more well known depictions of the famed statesman. Franklin's extraordinary life was unusual in many ways, including its length. Attaining the age of eighty-four, as he did, was uncommon in colonial times.

Franklin's death, "No other town burying its great men buried more of itself than Philadelphia with Franklin."[1]

Somber reminders of the city's loss were everywhere. Bells in churches and halls were muffled with cloth, giving their toll a mournful, hollow sound. In the harbor all

In his book Benjamin Franklin: The New American, *Milton Meltzer writes:*

"We feel we could be comfortable with [Franklin] at our table as we never could with the aristocratic George Washington, the intellectual Thomas Jefferson, or the starchy John Adams. He seems to be the most agreeable of persons in the intellectual Hall of Fame."

of the ships' flags were lowered out of respect. In New York, the capital of the new United States, the House of Representatives voted unanimously to wear black badges of mourning for a month. Across the United States flags were dropped to half-staff as a symbol of the nation's grief.

On every Philadelphia street corner, in every tavern and shop, people gathered and read to one another the *Gazette* article by Dr. John Jones, Franklin's physician. Jones went into detail about the last hours of the great man's life and the medical facts of the case.

"He Would Have Laughed"

The funeral itself was like nothing the United States had ever seen. More than twenty thousand people followed the funeral procession—the largest crowd that had ever gathered in America.

Witnesses declared that the mourners made up a mass of people over one-half mile long. At the front of the procession were all of Philadelphia's clergy, from every denomination. Dressed in their most colorful robes and hats, some carried

scepters, others had plain brown walking sticks, and many carried open Bibles and chanted prayers.

Following the clergy was the casket, surrounded by all of Pennsylvania's dignitaries, from the chief justice to lawmakers and the president of Philadelphia's treasury.

In addition to the community's most powerful and influential, the working people of Philadelphia were represented at the funeral. Franklin had started out as a printer and proudly called himself a printer throughout his life. To honor him the printers of Philadelphia marched in a silent row, wearing the leather apron that was a symbol of their trade. Other tradespeople marched too—candlemakers, blacksmiths, carpenters.

"He was a friend of the working people," wrote a shoemaker named William Hobbs. "Franklin would probably have had more good fun with them than [the dignitaries] at the front of the parade. He knew most of them, I imagine. He would have laughed to see them all, I am certain that he would."[2]

The procession accompanied the casket to the grave site, in a corner of Christ Church in downtown Philadelphia. There Franklin was laid to rest beside his wife Deborah, who had died sixteen years before. To mark his grave was the simple marker he requested, "Benjamin and Deborah Franklin, 1790."

"Un Homme Est Mort"

As large and impressive as Benjamin Franklin's funeral was, as huge as the outpouring of affection and respect of Americans was, Franklin's death had significance well beyond American borders.

In Paris, France, the National Assembly heard moving tributes to Benjamin Franklin from some of its members. Comte de Mirabeau, a nobleman who had gotten to know Franklin well, urged his fellow Frenchmen to do away with the idea that governments could mourn only the deaths of generals or royalty. Mirabeau called the American "a mighty genius" who freed men from the fears of "thunderbolts and tyrants."

Another of Franklin's friends, a French scientist named Felix Vicq d'Azyr, said tearfully, *"Un homme est mort, et deux mondes sont en deuil"* ("A man is dead and two worlds grieve").[3] The French lawmakers were easily persuaded by such tributes and voted to observe a three-day period of solemn mourning in honor of Benjamin Franklin.

What Sort of Man?

Benjamin Franklin was never president of the United States. He was never a general, nor a military strategist. He was not even a good public speaker, preferring instead to write out his thoughts and have others read them aloud.

Nonetheless, Franklin was well known throughout the United States and most of Europe. Even during his lifetime French shops sold rings, medallions, cups, plates, and china plaques decorated with his likeness. His face was, as he joked, "as familiar as the Moon."[4]

A Friend to Humankind

Franklin's colleague John Adams was often critical of Franklin but admired him for his wide reputation as this quote from Milton Meltzer's book Benjamin Franklin: The New American *reveals.*

"[His reputation] was more universal than that of Leibnitz or Newton, Frederick or Voltaire, and his character more beloved and esteemed than any or all of them. . . . His name was familiar to government and people, to kings and courtiers, nobility, clergy and philosophers, as well as plebeians, to such a degree that there was scarcely a peasant or citizen, coachman or footman, a lady's chambermaid or a scullion [helper] in a kitchen who was not familiar with it, and who did not consider him as a friend to human kind."

What was it about Benjamin Franklin that evoked so much affection and respect? Certainly Franklin was esteemed as one of the founding fathers of America. His contributions to the writing of both the Declaration of Independence and the Constitution were important.

He was also a diplomat. Many historians believe that the American colonies could never have won the Revolutionary War had it not been for the assistance of the French. And the one American sent to Paris to enlist their support was Benjamin Franklin.

In addition to his political side Benjamin Franklin had a scientific side. His contributions to the study of electricity are legendary. So, too, are his inventions—bifocals, the odometer, and the glass harmonica, to name just a few.

Franklin was a gifted writer, too. His famous *Autobiography, Poor Richard's Almanack,* and hundreds of editorials established him as one of the most widely read authors of the eighteenth century.

It is difficult to put a single label on Franklin, for he accomplished as much in his long lifetime as several more ordinary people could in theirs combined. One of the best-known biographers of Franklin, Carl Van Doren, dubbed Franklin "a harmonious human multitude."[5]

It was not just that Franklin lived during a time that gave him opportunities for such greatness. As Van Doren writes, "In any age, in any place, Franklin would have been great. Mind and will, talent and art, strength and ease, wit and grace met in him as if nature had been lavish and happy when he was shaped."[6]

Larger than Life?

Praise such as Van Doren's, although deserved, has had a negative effect on history's view of Franklin. It has made the man seem larger than life, too good to be true. "If one

Franklin the diplomat is hailed by the townspeople upon returning from his mission to France.

Franklin was a statesman, scientist, and inventor. Here he plays an armonica, a musical instrument he invented. The instrument became quite popular in Europe.

looks simply at the accomplishments of the man," wrote historian Thomas Altwood, "he is as remote as can be. How can anyone understand a human being who did so many valuable things, in so many different areas? He is unapproachable."[7]

American humorist Mark Twain poked fun at Franklin for this very thing in his essay, "The Late Benjamin Franklin." Twain complains that Franklin's accomplishments were so famous and so respected, and that he was so industrious and hardworking, that parents everywhere expected their own children to be the same. Twain writes that Franklin's

simplest acts . . . were contrived with a view to their being held up for the emulation of boys forever—boys who might otherwise have been happy. With a malevolence which is without parallel in history, he would work all day, and then sit up nights, and let on to be studying algebra by the light of a smoldering

No Presidential Mourning for Franklin

After Franklin's death the House of Representatives wore mourning for a month. In this quote taken from Meltzer's biography of Franklin, Thomas Jefferson expresses surprise that George Washington would not.

"I proposed to General Washington that the executive department should wear mourning; he declined it, because he said he would not know where to draw the line if he once began that ceremony. . . . I told him that the world had drawn so broad a line between him and Dr. Franklin, on the one side, and the residue of mankind on the other, that we might wear mourning for them, and the question still remain new and undecided as to all others. He thought it best, however, to avoid it."

fire, so that all other boys might have to do that also, or else have Benjamin Franklin thrown up to them.[8]

But, as Twain implied, Benjamin Franklin was more than just a grand total of accomplishments, inventions, and discoveries. He was a remarkable man, but human nonetheless.

He made mistakes—some very costly ones—in both his public and private lives. Some of these mistakes resulted in a lot of embarrassment, pain, and hurt, which he never was able to resolve. But these mistakes do not diminish Franklin; instead they allow him his humanity, making him seem more real, more alive.

Answering the questions Who was Benjamin Franklin? and Why was he important? is far more interesting when Franklin is allowed his mistakes as well as his remarkable achievements.

1 A Boston Boyhood

Even though Philadelphia would later claim him as a native son, Benjamin Franklin was actually born and raised in Boston. He was born on January 17, 1706, in an old, white house that his parents rented on Milk Street, near downtown Boston.

Though Philadelphia claimed him as a native son, Benjamin Franklin was born in this Boston house on January 17, 1706. He was fifteenth in a family of seventeen children, the son of an English cloth dyer who had come to America seeking religious freedom.

Fifteenth of Seventeen

Benjamin was born into a large family. His father, Josiah, had seven children from his first marriage. Josiah's second wife, Abiah, bore ten more children, Benjamin being the eighth—the fifteenth child in a family of seventeen children!

Although by today's standards such a family seems astonishingly large, in eighteenth-century Boston it was not unusual. Families with lots of children considered themselves lucky, for even though youngsters required plenty of supervision when small, they were useful as they grew older. Each child meant one more set of hands to help on the family farm or in the father's business.

From England to the Sign of the Blue Ball

Josiah Franklin's business was that of soap and candle making. Like most others in the American colonies, Josiah had come from England. He had come to America to worship freely and in his own way. In England he had been a religious dissenter whose ideas were different from those of the Church of England.

Josiah Franklin left England in 1683, while in his twenties. He had been a silk dyer in England and had hoped to continue his trade in America. He soon learned, however, that dyers were not as heavily in demand in Boston. After struggling financially for months as a dyer, Josiah finally gave up that trade and opened the small candle and soapmaking shop on Milk Street. The sign hanging outside of his shop was a blue ball, the symbol of the candle-making trade. His business grew and prospered over the years, and when Benjamin was six his father was able to move his business and family to a new location at the corner of Union and Hanover streets. The elder Franklin hoped that someday some of his sons would join him in the business.

Swim Fins and Kites

Young Benjamin still had years to go before he would be forced to make a decision about his future career. He spent his days playing with the other children in his large family. And in Boston, the largest city and busiest port in all of North America, there was plenty to do.

Boston was virtually surrounded by water—in fact, the city was connected to the rest of Massachusetts by a mile-long neck of swamp and lowlands. The place was ideal for Benjamin and his friends, who enjoyed nothing more than playing in and around the water.

In his autobiography Franklin remembered how much fun he had had as a

British warships (foreground) sail into Boston Harbor in 1768. Nearly surrounded by water, Boston provided young Ben Franklin ample opportunities to swim and sail, both of which he excelled at.

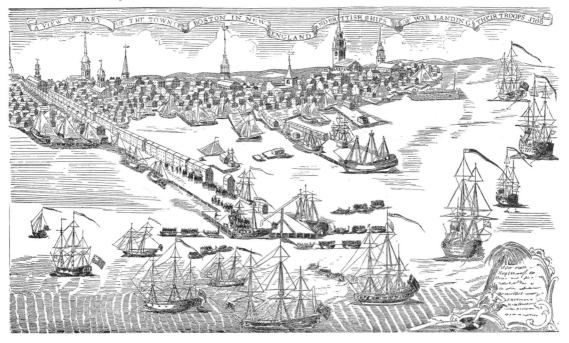

Showing early signs of his innate leadership abilities, young Ben (right) directs his friends in the building of a wharf. Franklin had fond memories of his childhood days playing on Boston's seashore.

child. "Living near the water, I was much in and about it, learned early to swim well, and to manage boats; and when in a boat or canoe with other boys, I was commonly allowed to govern [steer], especially in any case of difficulty."[9]

Benjamin's early love of swimming, in fact, spawned one of his first inventions. A fast and sure swimmer, he was eager to swim even faster. He tackled the problem by inventing what were probably the first swim fins. "I made two oval pallets," Franklin wrote, "each about ten inches long, and six broad, with a hole for the thumb, in order

to retain it fast in the palm of the hand. They much resembled a painter's pallets. In swimming I pushed the edges of these forward, and I struck the water with their flat surfaces as I drew them back."[10]

Franklin noted that he was able to swim faster but that the pallets were heavy and made his wrists tired. To increase his speed even more he fashioned a kind of webbed sandal for his feet. These, too, increased his speed but were cumbersome and difficult.

"I was not satisfied with them," he wrote much later in a letter to a French scientist friend, "because I observed that the stroke is partly given by the inside of the feet and the ankles, and not entirely with the soles of the feet."[11]

In another incident young Franklin was fascinated by the possibilities of using a kite while swimming. Flying a kite while floating on his back, he realized in surprise that the kite was pulling him quickly through the water. In an attempt to see how far the kite would take him, Benjamin had one of his friends take his clothes to the far side of the lake. Using his kite for power, and to the delight of his friends, Franklin made the crossing effortlessly.

"Don't Give Too Much for the Whistle"

Franklin's memories of his boyhood are mostly happy ones. However, one hard lesson stayed with him even through adulthood. When he was seven years old he was given a halfpenny to spend any way he wanted. "I went directly to a shop where they sold toys for children," remembered Franklin years later, "and being charmed with the sound of a whistle, that I met by the way in the hands of another boy, I voluntarily offered and gave all my money for one."

Franklin recalled that he was so happy with his purchase that he ran through his house, whistling as loud as he could. His excitement and pleasure were short-lived, however.

> My brothers and sisters, and cousins, understanding the bargain I had made, told me I had given four times as much for it as it was worth; put me in mind what good things I might have bought with the rest of my money; and laughed at me so much for my folly, that I cried with vexation; and the reflection gave me more chagrin than the whistle gave me pleasure.[12]

Franklin later claimed, though, that the incident had taught him a valuable lesson. He said that as a grown man, when he was tempted to buy something that was not really necessary, he would say to himself, Don't give too much for the whistle. By remembering that long-ago lesson, he would usually decide to save his money.

Almost a Tithe

Although Benjamin enjoyed a fun and carefree childhood, it ended early, as was the custom in those days. By the time children in eighteenth-century America were eight or nine, they needed to decide on their future careers. For children of farmers there was no real choice: sons became farmers themselves; daughters became farmers' wives. But in a city like Boston there were many trades, many choices.

Josiah Franklin noted that his son Benjamin was a quick learner and was especially fond of reading. The elder Franklin thought that Benjamin would

The Art of Diplomatic Persuasion

In his autobiography Franklin recalls that, as a boy, he was intrigued with the Socratic method of argument, which taught that it was better to persuade with questions and gentle comments than with confrontation.

"I continued this method for some few years, but gradually left it, retaining only the habit of expressing myself in terms of modest diffidence, never using when I advance anything that may possibly be disputed, the words *certainly, undoubtedly* . . . but rather say, I conceive, or I apprehend a thing to be so or so, it appears to me . . . or it is so, if I am not mistaken. This habit . . . has been of great advantage to me, when I have had occasion to . . . persuade men into measures that I have from time to time engaged in promoting."

make a good minister. It was the custom in those days for churchgoing people to tithe, or give one-tenth of their income back to the church. In large families where money was tight, parents would sometimes tithe their tenth son to the church, "giving" him to the church as a minister. This is precisely what Josiah Franklin decided to do.

He enrolled Benjamin in the Boston Latin School. The school was a good starting place for boys who were to become ministers. The curriculum included intensive study of Latin and Greek—a must for clergy in those days. The teachers were strict and expected their pupils to study at least five hours a day after classes.

In spite of the difficult work Benjamin did extremely well. Midway through the first year he was at the head of his class. His teachers informed him that he could skip a grade when the next year started.

Changing Plans

Benjamin's father was having second thoughts. In Franklin's words, "But my father in the meantime, from a view of the expense of a college education which, having so large a family, he could not well afford, and the mean living many so educated were afterwards able to obtain . . . took me from the school, and sent me to a school for writing and arithmetic."[13]

The economics of Josiah Franklin's decision made sense. The Latin School was expensive, but after that would come Harvard College (where most would-be ministers went). The costs of this further education, especially to a candle and soap maker, were staggering. Apart from the ex-

pense Benjamin's father may have had other reasons for changing his mind about tithing his son to the church. Benjamin showed early signs of being less devout than was required of a future minister.

Many years later William Temple Franklin, the grandson of Benjamin Franklin, wrote down a story that was well known in their family. It concerned young Benjamin's impatience with prayers and graces said before meals.

· Benjamin had been helping as his father salted and cured large slabs of meat and put them in a large cask to preserve the food for the winter. Hoping to eliminate table grace, Benjamin had a suggestion, "I think, Father," said Benjamin, "if you were to say Grace over the whole cask—once and for all—it would be a vast saving of time."[14]

As historian Ronald Clark remarks, "It was hardly the remark expected of a devout young boy being prepared for the ministry. Josiah, who like the son was a practical man, knew that entrance to Harvard demanded a certain minimum of unquestioning devotion; a scholarship for which he almost certainly hoped, demanded more."[15]

It was no doubt because of a combination of these reasons that Benjamin was sent to a new school. His father hoped that he would learn enough to keep the accounts at his shop. Benjamin did well at the writing part of his lessons but failed arithmetic.

Disappointed, Josiah Franklin brought his ten-year-old son home. He would have no more of school; in fact those two years were the only formal education Franklin ever had. Josiah decided that Benjamin would be a chandler—a candle and soap maker—just like his father.

A Dreary Occupation

Being a chandler was neither interesting nor challenging. It was a trade that, unlike that of blacksmith or carpenter, required no special talent. It was hard, smelly, dreary work.

Candles of today are usually colorful and attractively scented. But the candles made in shops like Franklin's were made of tallow, a yellowish substance obtained from boiling mutton or beef fat. The work was greasy, and the smell rancid.

The soapmaking part of Franklin's business was no more appealing. The lye used to make the strong soaps of those days had a sharp, stinging smell. The soap maker who had to stand by the pot of boiling lye sometimes permanently lost his sense of smell from the constant exposure to the harsh lye.

Benjamin's jobs in the shop were varied. He had to boil the lye for soap, cut wicks for the candles, fill the molds with tallow, wait on customers, and do errands for his father. All the while he was expected to watch how his father made the soap and candles so that someday he could run the shop.

The hours were long. Benjamin and his father usually worked twelve or fourteen hours each day, six days a week. Even then their living was only adequate. As each month went by Benjamin became more restless. He was a smart, inquisitive boy, full of ideas about things. But in his father's shop there was need for only long, mindless labor, not creativity.

Josiah Franklin was sensitive enough to his son's needs to recognize Benjamin's unhappiness. Although he could have forced Benjamin to continue as his helper (many boys had no choice at all), Josiah decided instead to help his son find a trade that he would enjoy.

Josiah may also have worried that Ben would run away rather than continue in the shop. One of Josiah's other sons had already run away to sea and was killed in a storm. He could not bear the thought of that happening again, and Benjamin knew it. In his autobiography Franklin wrote, "But my dislike to the trade continuing, my father was under apprehensions that if he did not find [a new trade] for me more agreeable, I should break away and get to sea, as his son Josiah had done to his great vexation."[16]

Together father and son walked the streets of Boston, watching tradesmen at their work. They observed carpenters, roofers, blacksmiths, joiners, and bricklayers. Josiah patiently explained to his son the various methods used by the different tradesmen in their work.

Deciding

None of the trades seemed right for him, although Benjamin did gain a healthy respect for the work that tradesmen did. "It has ever since been a pleasure to me," wrote Franklin later, "to see good workmen handle their tools; and it has been useful to me, having learned so much by it, as to be able to do little jobs myself in my house, when a workman could not readily be got."[17]

Benjamin did not decide on a trade until he was twelve years old. His brother James, nine years older than he, had just returned from England where he had been training to be a printer. He offered to take Benjamin on as an apprentice in his business.

A young Ben Franklin (center) at work in the candle-making shop. Franklin found his father's trade boring and sought to learn a different one. Unable to find a trade that interested him, he became an apprentice to his brother, a printer.

Being an apprentice was the best way to learn a trade in those days, although it was a long process. The apprentice was legally bound to the tradesman by signing an indenture (contract). The indenture usually guaranteed the apprentice a place to live and free meals, in addition to being taught a craft. In return the apprentice was required to work for the tradesman until he turned twenty-one and, in the meantime, to follow all the tradesman's instructions and orders.

It was a large commitment on Benjamin's part, and he signed the indenture with mixed emotions. He dreaded having the next nine years laid out for him with no choices. On the other hand he recognized that he probably would not get a better offer. The printing business was a good choice for someone who loved books and reading as much as he. The subject of the books did not seem to matter to Benjamin. He read theological works, historical essays—anything.

"From a child I was fond of reading," Franklin wrote, "and all the little money that came into my hands was ever laid out in books."[18] The thought of working in a shop that printed pamphlets and other reading material no doubt seemed like an exciting prospect.

Printer's Apprentice

Like his work in his father's candle-making shop, Benjamin's work as a printer's apprentice was difficult. At first his jobs were easy ones, keeping a fire going in the fireplace and running errands for his brother. He watched closely as James selected individual metal letters from a tray, and stacked them, line by line, onto the bed of the press.

Once the type was arranged large leather rollers were used to coat the type with sticky ink. Sheets of paper were placed on a frame and fed into the press so they could be stamped with the lines of type. Hours of work went into the printing of just one page of type.

James was good at his work: even so, business was usually slow. In a town the size of Boston (with a population of about twelve thousand), only so much printing business was available. And competition was steep—there were three printers in Boston besides James.

James's shop printed pamphlets and handbills. It even did a lot of printing of linen, calico, and silk fabrics. In an advertisement for the printing shop, James promised that he could print the fabric "in good figures, very lively and durable colors, and without the offensive smell which commonly attends the linens printed here."[19]

"I Escaped Being a Poet"

As interesting as printing was to Benjamin, he was finding that he enjoyed writing, too. He was just thirteen when he began experimenting with rhythm and rhyme, and he wrote two poems. He was quite proud of them and showed them to his brother.

The first was dramatic and sad. Called "The Lighthouse Tragedy," it was based on a true incident: the keeper of a new lighthouse in Boston's outer harbor had recently been swept to his death, along with his wife and daughter. The second poem

Terms of an Apprenticeship

The formal indenture agreement between Benjamin Franklin and his brother James was typical. This excerpt from the agreement is taken from Carl Van Doren's biography of Franklin.

The twelve-year-old promised to "put himself apprentice to his brother, to learn his art, and with him, after the manner of an apprentice, to serve. During which term, the said apprentice his master faithfully shall or will serve, his secrets keep, his lawful commands everywhere do. . . . Taverns, inns, or alehouses he shall not haunt. At cards, dice, tables, or any unlawful game he shall not play. Matrimony he shall not contract; nor from the service of his said master day or night absent himself."

Franklin works in the print shop. At age twelve he contracted to be his brother's apprentice for nine years. The position afforded him the opportunity to read and write, skills that he put to good use.

was a kind of drinking song to be sung in taverns and inns. It was called "A Sailor's Song on the Taking of Teach or Blackbeard the Pirate."

The poems received mixed reviews from his family. James, always eager to drum up new business, printed the poems and sent Benjamin out into the streets to sell them. Josiah Franklin, however, was far less supportive.

In his autobiography Franklin wrote, "My father discouraged me, by ridiculing my Performances, and telling me Verse-Makers were generally Beggars; so I escaped being a poet, most probably a very bad one."[20]

Saving Money

Benjamin stopped writing poetry, but he continued to enjoy reading. There were no public libraries in America in those days; Benjamin had to borrow books from his father's or James's personal libraries. Sometimes, too, generous customers in the print shop offered to lend Benjamin books. There were also bookstores, but the books were too expensive for an unsalaried apprentice to purchase.

When he was sixteen Benjamin hit on an idea that would give him some much-needed pocket money with which to buy the books he wanted. The idea came from one of the books he had read—*The Way To Wealth,* by Thomas Tryon. The book stressed the benefits of a vegetarian diet. The author claimed that by not eating meat one would be healthier, more clearheaded, and could live more cheaply. Intrigued, Benjamin decided to become a vegetarian. That proved to be surprisingly difficult.

As the master of several apprentices James was responsible for providing room and board for his students. Since he was not married, and therefore could not provide meals himself, James paid a family in town to feed his apprentices. The meals were plentiful but consisted largely of meat. When he refused to eat the meat, Benjamin was loudly criticized.

Benjamin then asked James if he would be willing to pay *him* half the money James spent on boarding him, and then Benjamin would be responsible for buying his own meals. James agreed, for it would save him money. Benjamin found very quickly that the new system benefited him in more ways than one.

When James and the other apprentices went to meals, Benjamin remained at the shop. He enjoyed the quiet time to himself and used it to read. He found, too, that he required less food than he imagined, "often no more than a biscuit or a slice of bread, a handful of raisins or a tart from the pastry cook's, and a glass of water," he remembered years later.[21] And with the money he saved he was able to buy more books.

Self-Taught

Some of the books Benjamin chose were to help him learn subjects he knew nothing about. Having been embarrassed at his failure in mathematics in school, for example, Benjamin wrote, "I took Cocker's book of arithmetic, and went through the whole by myself with great ease. I also read Seller's and Sturmy's books of navigation, and became acquainted with the little Geometry they contain."[22]

However, the most important part of Benjamin's self-instruction was his systematic approach to learning to write. "Prose writing has been of great use to me in the course of my life," he later wrote in his autobiography, "and was a principal means of my advancement."[23]

Benjamin devised an interesting way to learn to write. He had found a volume of *The Spectator*, a London newspaper famous for its satirical writing. Fascinated, he read and reread one of the essays. He made notes about the construction of each paragraph, trying to understand what made the writing so good.

He put his notes aside for a few days and then, without looking at the newspaper essay, tried to imitate what he had read—and with interesting results. "By comparing my work afterwards with the original," Franklin wrote later, "I discovered many faults and amended them; but I sometimes had the pleasure of fancying that . . . I had been lucky enough to improve the method

Young Franklin studies in his room by candlelight. He taught himself many subjects, including mathematics, at which he had failed miserably during two short years of formal education.

or the language, and this encouraged me to think I might possibly in time come to be a tolerable English writer, of which I was extremely ambitious."[24]

The *New England Courant*

Benjamin's opportunity to show just how well he could write came very soon. In 1721, when Benjamin was fifteen years old, his brother James decided to start a newspaper. He named it the *New England Courant,* after a well-known English newspaper, the *London Courant.*

The *Courant* was not the first newspaper in Boston. There were two others, the *Boston Gazette* and the *Boston News Letter.* Both of these newspapers were published by postmasters, who had a financial advantage, for they didn't have to pay postage for the delivery of their papers. In addition, postmasters in the colonies had access to news from England before other citizens. Their newspapers could beat anyone else's in the reporting of such news items.

But they were such boring news items! Many were simply reprinted bits from European newspapers, telling which foreign diplomat was received by which embassy at a state dinner, or the names of ships, their captains, and the arrival and departure times. The "news" was hardly new, for it took three or four months for European news to trickle into the colonies.

James Franklin was not worried by this type of competition. He felt that as a private citizen, not a government-appointed postmaster, *he* had an advantage. He did not have to worry about offending the governor or any other high-ranking officials

The front page of James Franklin's newspaper, the first independent colonial newspaper. Unknown to his brother, young Benjamin wrote satirical articles for the paper under the name Silence Dogood. The articles lampooned the authorities and advocated equal rights for women.

and losing his position, as a postmaster might. He wanted to print real news that affected people in the American colonies, news that was local.

He also hoped to have some fun. James and some of his friends wrote essays and articles criticizing the government and church leaders, who they felt were much stricter than the ones back in England. To protect themselves from being singled out by those officials, they did not use their own names. Instead, they used humorous names like Ichabod Henroost, Fanny Mournful, and Tabatha Talkative.

Franklin (left) discusses business with customers in his brother's print shop. Indentured for nine years as an apprentice, Franklin was able to free himself from the contract after five years. He soon found himself leaving Boston for New York and, then, Philadelphia.

The *New England Courant* was the first independent newspaper in the American colonies. The paper was modest, for it was only a single sheet, printed on both sides. The circulation at first was small, too, with just a few hundred readers. But as more people were entertained by the satire and humor of the writing, the paper gained in popularity.

Silence Dogood

Benjamin listened to James and his friends as they eagerly planned each issue of the *Courant*. He wanted to try his hand at writing a satiric essay but worried about being refused by his brother. Secrecy seemed to be the best solution. Disguising his handwriting and slipping his essay under the print shop door at night, Benjamin submitted a phony letter from a woman he named Silence Dogood.

James and his friends at the *Courant* loved the essay. To Benjamin's delight James and the others spent hours in the print shop discussing how well it was written and who Silence Dogood might be. Franklin later wrote, "I had the exquisite pleasure of finding [that my letter] met with their approbation, and that in their different guesses at the author, none were named but men of some character among us for learning and ingenuity."[25]

Ruffling Feathers

Benjamin wrote thirteen more letters in Silence Dogood's name, each one more entertaining than the last. She poked fun at religious hypocrites, the town drunks, and prestigious Harvard University. She advocated equal rights for girls and women and freedom of speech.

Benjamin kept the whole affair a secret from James until he had written the last letter. When he finally broke the news to his brother, James was furious. He felt that Benjamin, a mere apprentice, had upstaged him in front of his colleagues (who were delighted that Benjamin had composed the letters), and this would not be tolerated.

"I began," wrote Franklin later, "to be considered a little more by my brother's acquaintances and in a manner that did not quite please him, as he thought, probably with reason, that it tended to make me too vain."[26]

James did not have much time to worry about being bested by his little brother. He soon had more important problems. James wrote an editorial for the newspaper that soundly criticized the Massachusetts government authorities. Officials had been irritated by the *Courant*'s stories more than once, and this seemed to be a good occasion to teach James a lesson. Without so much as a trial, James was thrown into prison.

He was released a little more than a month later, after promising to make his newspaper less controversial. However, it wasn't long before another article in the paper aroused the anger of Boston officials. This time James's punishment was more severe. And it was the beginning of free life for his brother Benjamin.

Publisher—and Runaway

The Massachusetts legislature told James that he was no longer allowed to go on publishing the *New England Courant*. However, there was nothing in the legislature's decision that said the *Courant* couldn't be published under someone else's name.

That is just what happened. James continued to put out the newspaper, but under his brother Benjamin's name. To make the whole thing look official, James signed Benjamin's old indenture papers,

An Introduction

Young Benjamin took over his brother's paper the New England Courant *for a while, and in the February 23, 1723 issue had a chance to write his first editorial.*

"The present undertaking . . . is designed purely for the diversion and merriment of the reader. Pieces of pleasancy and mirth have a secret charm in them to allay the heats and tumors of our spirits, and to make a man forget his restless resentments. . . . The main design of this weekly paper will be to entertain the town with the most comical and diverting incidents of humane life."

swearing that the boy was released from the four years of apprenticeship that remained.

Of course James had no intention of freeing Benjamin. He made Benjamin sign new, secret papers of indenture. But Benjamin knew that his brother was in a sticky situation. He would never dare show those new indenture papers to force Benjamin back to work.

Benjamin had worked hard. He had learned a great deal while working in the print shop. But he was restless after five years of being an apprentice. He wanted to see more of the world than the little print shop in Boston.

A friend helped him sell his books to raise a little money. The friend convinced the captain of a boat bound for New York to take Benjamin on board. At the age of seventeen Benjamin Franklin was virtually penniless and on his way to a city where he knew no one. But he was free.

2 A Rising Star

Three days after his boat set sail from Boston, Benjamin reached New York. But he was disappointed, for there was no work for a young printer in that town. People he met in New York advised him to move on to Philadelphia, where he might find a job in a print shop there.

His Philadelphia Arrival

The teenager had very little money with which to get to Philadelphia. The fastest way would have been to take another boat, but it was too expensive, and Benjamin had no guarantee of a job once he reached his destination. Instead, he traveled across New Jersey on foot, slogging through wetlands and sludge in a heavy rain for fifty miles. He went the rest of the way in a rowboat down the Delaware River with several others—each taking their turn at the oars.

Benjamin's arrival in Philadelphia was somewhat comical, as he later remembered. He was wet, dirty, and very tired. He had a penny in his pocket and bought three, large, puffy rolls from a baker and carried one under each arm while munching on the third. He recalled how a young woman had smiled as she watched him

from her front porch, "she, standing at the door, saw me, and thought I made—as I certainly did—a most awkward, ridiculous appearance."[27]

Benjamin tried to find work as soon as possible. He made the rounds of all the

Seventeen-year-old Ben Franklin upon his arrival in Philadelphia. He carries a baker's roll under each arm—all he could afford after his long trip by foot and rowboat from New York.

Franklin described himself as having a "most awkward, ridiculous appearance" upon his arrival in Philadelphia. The young woman watching him walk by is Deborah Read, whom Franklin later married.

town printers the next morning and found one who would give him a job. The man's name was Samuel Keimer, and he was the strangest fellow Benjamin had ever met.

Keimer was, according to Franklin, "an odd fish; ignorant of common life." He was filthy and unkempt, "slovenly to extreme dirtiness," with long, greasy hair and a beard like Moses.[28] Benjamin knew far more than Keimer did about printing. But Keimer was an interesting man and loved to argue about religion, philosophy, and other topics Benjamin was interested in, so they got along quite well.

Keimer lived in a house with no furniture—a fact that young Benjamin found astonishing. Because he could not provide lodging for his new assistant, Keimer found Benjamin a room in the house of John Read. Read's daughter Deborah was the same young woman who had found Benjamin's entrance into the city so amusing.

His Own Epitaph

When he was about twenty-two years old, Franklin composed his own epitaph. It was written tongue in cheek, although there were some who felt Franklin would really have wanted it inscribed on his tombstone.

"The body of
B. Franklin, Printer,
(Like the Cover of an old Book
Its Contents torn out
And stript of its Lettering and Gilding.)
Lies here, Food for Worms.
But the Work shall not be lost;
For it will, (as he believed) appear once more,
Revised and corrected
By the Author."

Meeting the Governor

Benjamin had not been in Philadelphia more than a few months when he received a letter from his brother-in-law, Robert Holmes. Holmes, the captain of a trading ship, had heard rumors that Benjamin had come to Philadelphia. He wrote to Benjamin, reminding him of how worried his parents were and urging him to return to Boston—that all would be forgiven.

Benjamin wrote a long letter in response to his brother-in-law. He said that he did not

William Keith, colonial governor of Pennsylvania, took an interest in young Benjamin after reading a letter Franklin had written to a family member.

Franklin on an errand for Keimer's print shop, where he had found employment soon after arriving in Philadelphia. Though unkempt and eccentric, his new employer, like Franklin, enjoyed arguing about philosophy, religion, and other topics.

believe that he had done anything for which he needed forgiveness. He explained in detail why he had left Boston so that Holmes might relate it to Benjamin's family.

The letter had far-reaching effects. Robert Holmes received Benjamin's letter while the governor of Pennsylvania, Sir William Keith, was visiting him. Keith himself read Benjamin's letter and was quite impressed with both the style of Benjamin's writing and the bravery it took for Benjamin to set off on his own to Philadelphia.

Interested in helping Benjamin, the governor paid a visit to Keimer's print shop to meet the teenager. Keimer was flabbergasted when the most important man in the colony walked into his shop—and even more astonished when he asked to see Benjamin. "I was not a little surprised," Franklin later wrote, "and Keimer stared like a pig poisoned."[29]

Franklin arrived in Philadelphia in October 1723. In his Autobiography, he later described his rather "unlikely beginnings" in that city:

"I was in my working dress, my best clothes being to come round by sea. I was dirty from my journey; my pockets were stuffed out with shirts and stockings, and I knew no soul nor where to look for lodging. I was fatigued with traveling, rowing [he had helped navigate a rowboat on the last part of his journey], and want of rest. I was very hungry, and my whole stock of cash consisted of a Dutch dollar and about a shilling in copper."

A Proposition and a Reunion

Keith suggested to Benjamin that he go into business for himself, that he had more than enough skill to open his own print shop. The governor promised that, if Benjamin had his own shop, he would make sure that Benjamin got government printing jobs—more than enough work to become successful. What Benjamin needed, then, was money to buy presses and other equipment so that he could open his business.

Keith urged Benjamin to get financial support for the business from his father. Keith even wrote a letter to Josiah Franklin, outlining his proposal. Benjamin was flattered and excited and made arrangements to sail as soon as possible back to Boston to request the funds.

Josiah Franklin was delighted to see his son. The whole family, in fact, gave him a hero's welcome—all except his brother James. James acted sullen and jealous, perhaps resentful that Benjamin had returned in a "genteel new suit from head to foot, a watch, and [his] pockets lined with near five pounds sterling in silver."[30]

The elder Franklin read the letter from the governor but was not impressed. He told his son that an eighteen-year-old was far too young to open his own business. He should still be learning from an older printer, not making decisions on his own. Although he was proud of what his son had accomplished thus far, Josiah Franklin told his son that no, he would not put up the money for a new printing business in Philadelphia.

A Decision to Leave

Benjamin returned to Philadelphia empty-handed to resume working as Samuel Keimer's printing assistant. But Governor Keith was persistent. He believed that Benjamin's talents were being wasted in Keimer's shop, with its shabby, worn-out equipment.

Keith contacted Benjamin again, and this time he made a more attractive offer.

He declared that he would provide financial backing himself. He told Benjamin to compile a list of all the materials and supplies he would need to start a print shop of his own. This done, Keith would see to it that there would be funds to buy the materials.

Still flattered by the governor's attention, Benjamin made up the list and showed it to Keith. The governor suggested that Benjamin sail to London to purchase the equipment. He assured Benjamin that he would provide the letters of credit so that Benjamin would not have to pay for a thing. In addition, Keith would write letters of introduction to some influential business people in London, the sort of people that Benjamin would enjoy meeting.

Benjamin booked passage on a ship sailing for London. His first trip—from Boston to Philadelphia by way of New York—had been interesting, but this new adventure promised to be more exciting than anything he had ever done.

As the day of his departure grew nearer, Benjamin became nervous. The letters of credit and introduction from Keith had not arrived. However, the governor assured him that there was nothing to worry about, that the letters would be delivered directly to the ship. He "wished me heartily a good voyage and a speedy return," wrote Franklin.[31]

Promises Broken

Benjamin's nervousness about the letters turned out to be well founded. As the ship sailed Benjamin found to his dismay that there were no letters from Governor Keith. A kindly Quaker merchant noticed the downhearted boy and struck up a conversation.

The merchant, whose name was Thomas Denham, was somewhat acquainted with Governor Keith. He told Benjamin that most likely there had been no letters of introduction for him. As for letters of credit to help purchase the printing presses and materials in London, they, too, were surely nonexistent, for the governor had no credit at all.

Benjamin was confused and hurt. How could the governor have led Benjamin on when he had no intention of helping him in his business? It was only after many years that he could understand that Keith had not done what he did out of meanness or spite. Instead, the governor was a dreamer, an idea man, with very little to back up his dreams. "He wished to please everybody," wrote Franklin in his autobiography, "and having little to give, he gave expectations."[32]

Understanding Keith's motives could not have helped Benjamin as he got off the ship in London. He was stranded in England, with no one to give him shelter or meals. He had very little money—not enough for a ticket home to Philadelphia.

The Water American

Just as Benjamin had been able to rely on his trade for work when he first went to Philadelphia, here too he was confident. He was a printer—and a good one. London in the early 1700s was a printing center of Europe; there were scores of publishing houses that needed good printers. In less than a week after his arrival in

A section of eighteenth-century London. A center of the European printing trade, London offered Franklin many employment and learning opportunities. He soon distinguished himself among his peers.

London, Benjamin had found work at Samuel Palmer's print shop. After a few months at Palmer's he landed an even better job at the printing house of James Watt.

It did not take Benjamin long to stand out among his fellow printers at Watt's. For one thing, he was much stronger than the others. While the other printers, some taller and broader shouldered than he, could carry only one heavy frame of type at a time, Benjamin had no difficulty with two. He had a careful eye and worked more quickly in setting rows of type.

When asked about his strength and speed, Benjamin suggested to his fellow workers that they might be slowed down by the large amounts of beer they drank. "We had an alehouse boy who attended always in the house to supply the workmen," wrote Franklin later. "My companion at the press drank every day a pint before breakfast, a pint at breakfast, with his bread and cheese, a pint between breakfast and dinner, a pint at dinner, a pint in the afternoon about six o'clock, and another when he had done his day's work."[33]

Benjamin told his fellow workers that there was no more strength in a quart of beer than in a penny's worth of bread. He advised them to buy the bread and drink water, as he did. He felt clearheaded and saved money besides.

For this the printers called Benjamin the "Water American." Although they teased him, it was out of kindness. He was no snob who looked down at the workingmen as if he were better than they. To the contrary, Benjamin was a friendly, outgoing young man who was quick with a compliment and always eager to learn. And his talents at the press were obvious. If drinking water helped, some of his companions in the shop were even willing to give it a try!

There may have been another reason Benjamin was known as the Water American—his great swimming ability. He had taught a couple of the printers how to swim, and one afternoon when they were all visiting some friends in the country, he was urged to show off his talents. He wrote later:

At the request of the company, I stripped and leaped into the river, and swam from near Chelsea to Blackfryars [a distance of more than three miles], performing on the way many feats of activity both upon and under water that surprised and pleased those to whom they were novelties.[34]

His reputation as a swimmer became so great, in fact, that several wealthy Londoners suggested that he open a swimming school so that he could teach their children how to swim. Although he could have made a good deal of money in such a business, Benjamin declined the idea, for he was thinking more and more of returning home to Philadelphia.

Sir Isaac Newton, perhaps the greatest scientist of his day, was only one of many famous historical figures living and working in London at the same time young Ben Franklin lived there. Because of his involvement in the printing business, Franklin had access to the principal philosophical discussions of his day.

London in Its Golden Age

Benjamin's eagerness to return to America was not a reflection on London. In fact, he thought it the most interesting place he had ever seen.

London of the 1720s was in a sort of golden age. England was at peace with her perennial enemy, France, so there seemed to be no shortage of money. Business and trade flourished, as did literature and the growing field of science. In England at this time Sir Isaac Newton was putting forth his scientific theories. Writers such as Jonathan Swift and Daniel Defoe were making their marks, too.

Although the teenager from America was certainly not included in the exciting academic circles of London, he was closer to them than he would have been in Philadelphia or Boston. And as a printer Benjamin often was able to read new books and theories before they were published. He was especially fascinated by how many different philosophies there were about politics and government.

Benjamin even tried his own hand at philosophy. In 1725 he wrote a short book entitled *A Dissertation on Liberty and Necessity, Pleasure and Pain,* which he then printed. His employer at the print shop, according to biographer Carl Van Doren, thought Benjamin's ideas "abominable." Even so, the man noticed that Benjamin had the mind and the skill to go far as a writer.

An Idea and a Ticket Home

There is no way of knowing what Benjamin would have done had he not had a visit from Thomas Denham, the merchant he had met on the ship from Philadelphia. Denham was a wealthy man, and he now hoped that with the help of young Benjamin Franklin he might become wealthier.

Denham wanted to open a store in Philadelphia. He recognized that Benjamin had good sense and a clever mind and wanted to train the young man in the business. He could start out as clerk at the modest salary of fifty pounds a year. However, all the while he clerked he would be learning the details of the business and would soon be earning fat commissions.

The idea sounded good to Benjamin, who missed Philadelphia in spite of the excitement of London. The two shook hands on the deal. Within the month Denham had purchased tickets for both, and they sailed for Philadelphia.

A Curious Mind

During the eight-week journey on board the ship in the summer of 1726, Franklin kept a journal. That journal is interesting to historians, for in it he wrote down hundreds of things he observed. His mind never rested, it seems. He wrote about the weather, the fish he spotted on the journey, and the idiosyncrasies of the crew and his fellow passengers.

With a scientist's eye he noticed the Gulf Stream, the powerful river that runs in the ocean from the Gulf of Mexico across the Atlantic. He noted in his journal that it was a phenomenon worth studying. He gave detailed descriptions of the vegetation that grew in the water and the various crabs and shellfish.

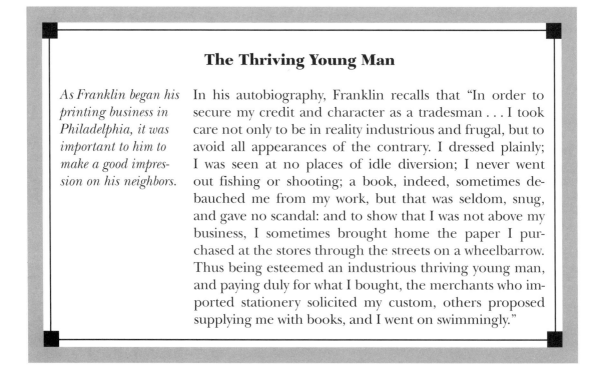

The Thriving Young Man

As Franklin began his printing business in Philadelphia, it was important to him to make a good impression on his neighbors.

In his autobiography, Franklin recalls that "In order to secure my credit and character as a tradesman . . . I took care not only to be in reality industrious and frugal, but to avoid all appearances of the contrary. I dressed plainly; I was seen at no places of idle diversion; I never went out fishing or shooting; a book, indeed, sometimes debauched me from my work, but that was seldom, snug, and gave no scandal: and to show that I was not above my business, I sometimes brought home the paper I purchased at the stores through the streets on a wheelbarrow. Thus being esteemed an industrious thriving young man, and paying duly for what I bought, the merchants who imported stationery solicited my custom, others proposed supplying me with books, and I went on swimmingly."

Besides reporting on his observations Franklin wrote many pages reflecting on his own life. He regretted that up until then his life had been like bad theater—"a confused variety of different scenes."[35] He had made mistakes in his dealings with his family and friends, he felt, but he was eager to do better.

Although there are some key pages missing from this journal, an important section remains. It is a list of rules that young Franklin intended to follow from that time on—a sort of New Year's resolution list. In the list he declared that he would be frugal, that he would always tell the truth, and that he would speak kindly of someone or not speak at all.

Although Franklin's goals seem unrealistic and impossible to follow, it is clear that he was desperately trying to establish an order that he felt was lacking from his life. When the ship docked in Philadelphia Benjamin Franklin was full of hope. He had a job. And more importantly, he had a plan that he felt would take him successfully through the rest of his life.

Chapter

3 A New Leaf

For the first weeks after Franklin returned to Philadelphia, his life seemed well ordered. True to his word, Thomas Denham had opened a store, and twenty-year-old Franklin was working as head clerk. Three months after the store opened Denham became very sick. Three months later he was dead, and the store closed. Once again Franklin had to fall back on his old trade, printing.

Two Partnerships

Franklin found work immediately with his old employer, Samuel Keimer. Keimer had not learned much about either business or printing during Franklin's absence, and the print shop was floundering. He offered to take Franklin on as a partner of sorts. Franklin would be the supervisor,

Looking north on Second Street in eighteenth-century Philadelphia. Franklin returned here from England to manage Denham's store, but six months later, events turned his path a different way.

In 1728 they opened the shop, but it was not long before it seemed that this partnership, too, was flawed. Hugh Meredith had little interest in learning to become a master printer. He was an alcoholic and preferred to spend his days in taverns drinking with his friends. But because Hugh's father was financing the business, Benjamin did not complain about the situation. He just managed the business as if he were the sole owner.

Eventually Hugh's father ran into financial trouble and could no longer pump money into the print shop. Not long afterward two wealthy business people approached Franklin with another deal. If he would get rid of Hugh, they said, they would gladly back him financially. Relieved to be through with printing, Hugh stepped down, and Benjamin was finally the sole owner of his own business.

Franklin discusses his wares with prospective customers in front of his print and book shop in Philadelphia. Fresh financial backing had allowed him to be sole owner of the shop.

the foreman who would train and manage the four young printers Keimer had hired.

Franklin's salary was good, and for a while it seemed that the arrangement might work well. However, after six months Keimer decided that he could save a lot of money by cutting Franklin's wages and relying more on the four printers who had now been so well trained.

Angry, Benjamin quit, taking Hugh Meredith with him. Meredith was one of Keimer's four printers, and he and Benjamin had become friends. Meredith's father was wealthy and offered to supply the money for the two young men to open their own shop.

The Birth of the *Gazette*

Business was slow for printers in Philadelphia. There were five or six in town, but only enough work to keep two or three busy. To increase business a creative printer needed to do some writing of his own.

Benjamin remembered how exciting it had been to work on his brother James's newspaper in Boston. He decided to start his own newspaper, and this time he could make all the decisions himself.

There was already one newspaper in Philadelphia, called the *American Weekly Mercury*. It was, in Franklin's words, "a paltry thing, wretchedly managed, and no way entertaining; and yet profitable to [its publisher]."[36] Franklin believed he could do far better, but before he had a chance he was beaten to it by none other than Samuel Keimer. Keimer gave his newspaper the unbelievably long name of the *Universal Instructor in all Arts and Sciences: and Pennsylvania Gazette.*

Keimer struggled with the newspaper as he had with his print shop. The articles were dull; many were copied word for word from an encyclopedia. After a run of less than a year Keimer's newspaper was floundering. He happily sold it to twenty-three-year-old Franklin for almost nothing. Ironically, it would be this newspaper that would make Benjamin one of the most influential, wealthy men in Philadelphia.

His Own Newspaper

The first thing Franklin did was change the newspaper's ridiculous name, shearing it to the *Pennsylvania Gazette.* With the new name came a fresh new format.

Using some of the tricks he had observed in James's *New England Courant*, Franklin wrote humorous letters from strange characters such as Anthony Afterwit, who told about his spend-happy wife who drove him into bankruptcy. Another was Cecilia Single, who complained that the editors of the *Gazette* favored men. No one believed that these letters were real, but they were entertaining and funny.

It was not just humor that sold newspapers. Besides being funny the *Gazette* was courageous in its no-nonsense articles about life in Pennsylvania. Franklin had observed with interest, for example, the quarreling between the royal governor of Pennsylvania and the colony's assembly.

The front page of Franklin's newspaper, the Pennsylvania Gazette, *January 15, 1739. The paper made Franklin one of the wealthiest, most influential men in Philadelphia.*

The royal governor was from England and was not chosen by the people of Pennsylvania. The assembly had thought it fair to pay the governor no fixed salary, but rather whatever they felt he deserved for his services; in that way they could maintain a little power over colony affairs. However, the governor objected, saying he wanted a set salary and did not wish his performance to be judged by the assembly at all.

Franklin jumped into the discussions with both feet. He wrote editorials supporting the assembly, noting that its members "still retain that ardent spirit of liberty, and that undaunted courage in the defense of it, which has in every age so gloriously distinguished Britons and Englishmen from all the rest of mankind." [37]

Sawdust and Water

Such issues of the *Gazette* were widely read throughout Pennsylvania and met with much interest—especially among the members of the assembly. Franklin himself benefited, for as historian Ronald Clark writes, "just as the papers of the nineteenth- and twentieth-century newspaper barons exercised influence in the wider social and political worlds, so did the *Gazette* steadily bring Franklin to an influential position in Pennsylvania."[38]

The print shop was given the contract to produce the paper currency for the colony. Soon afterwards the colonies of Delaware and New Jersey offered Franklin the job of printing their money, too. He was a visible, respected man in his community.

Along with fame and success came notoriety. By criticizing the royal governor Franklin was ruffling the feathers of some very prominent people—including the sons of William Penn, the founder of the colony.

Some of Franklin's backers warned him that he should tone down his editorials. To discuss the issue, he invited them to his house for dinner. He listened as they warned him that the *Gazette* would never succeed if he angered the Penns and their followers.

After they had had their say he served dinner. Franklin's guests watched as some strange, tan mixture was spooned into their bowls. Was it some kind of mush? It smelled funny, and when they tasted it they gagged. There was nothing else on the table but a pitcher of cold water.

Franklin's pamphlet on the need for a paper currency in Pennsylvania persuaded the colony's assembly and won him the job of printing the money. His five-pound note (right) featured an intricate, hard-to-copy leaf pattern to discourage counterfeiters.

The guests watched in awe as Franklin heaped a large helping into a bowl and soaked it down in cold water. He ate it as if it were delicious. They finally asked what it was they had been served.

"Sawdust-meal and water," Franklin said. "Now go tell the rest of Philadelphia that a man who can eat that for supper doesn't need to be beholden to anyone."[39]

"The Requirement Was a Wife"

In spite of his outspoken views on politics, Franklin's printing and newspaper business grew and flourished. By the end of the 1720s, says one historian, Franklin "needed only one addition to complete the picture of the up-and-coming Philadelphian. The requirement was a wife, and [he] set about filling it with his customary efficiency and zeal."[40]

In eighteenth-century America men often planned for marriage before deciding on a wife. And often the need for a wife had little to do with love or companionship. A dowry, money given to a man by his new wife's parents, was highly prized by young men starting out in business. Although Franklin's business was good, he still had debts to pay. The combination of cash and a wife seemed an attractive prospect.

Historians say that Franklin's need for money irritated the parents of one girl. He told her mother that he needed a little more than one hundred pounds, the equivalent of just over $400.00. "I let her know that I expected as much money with [a bride] as would pay off my remaining debt for the printing house," he later wrote.[41]

The woman told Franklin that she and her husband did not have that kind of money. Franklin suggested that they mortgage their house to pay the dowry. The par-

Philadelphia in 1729

Frederic Birmingham claimed in the April 1982 issue of The Saturday Evening Post *that, when Franklin began the* Gazette *in 1729, Philadelphia was far from being an important political center.*

"In 1729, the town of Philadelphia, created out of the wilderness in 1681 by William Penn's surveyor, was still a raw, backwoods settlement of only 7,000 people. Philly still had plenty of small game frisking about its unpaved streets. At night, the howls of wolves on the edge of town echoed through the dark streets and alleys. . . . It was this sleepy place which Franklin proposed to thrust into the mainstream of the other colonies and of the world beyond."

Deborah Read Franklin first saw Benjamin as he walked by her house upon his arrival in Philadelphia. They dated later, but she had married while he was living in London. She married Franklin after her first husband abandoned her.

However, he wrote to her while in London, telling her that he did not plan on returning soon to Philadelphia. It was, as he later admitted, one of the great mistakes of his life.

In despair over Franklin's long absence, Deborah had married a man named Rogers. He turned out to be a fortune hunter—taking the generous dowry from her parents and carousing with other women. No one knew for sure, but it was believed that Rogers had fled to the West Indies, and it was rumored that he had another wife there.

The bad marriage had taken its toll on Deborah. She seldom smiled and was painfully shy. She was delighted when Franklin finally proposed. They were married in a common-law ceremony in September 1730. A church wedding would have been forbidden because of the embarrassing possibilities that Rogers might return and that the rumors of another wife might be false.

ents refused and finally told him that their daughter was not a suitable match for him.

He finally married Deborah Read, the young woman in whose parents' house Franklin had stayed while he worked for Samuel Keimer. As eighteen-year-olds the two had been romantically involved. "I had a great respect and affection for [Deborah] and had some reason to believe she had the same for me," he later wrote. "But as I was about to take a long voyage, and we were both very young . . . it was thought most prudent by her mother to prevent our going too far at present."[42]

Although they had not become engaged back then, the two did have an agreement that they would renew their love when Franklin returned from London.

A Good and Faithful Helpmate

With Deborah to help him Franklin set about expanding his business. He added on a small shop that sold a little of everything—"from the salves and ointments concocted by Deborah's mother . . . to the crown soap made in Boston by Franklin's brother John according to a secret recipe."[43] There was also more common merchandise, such as stationery, ink, books, quills, sealing wax, and pounce, a powder used in those days to blot ink.

Besides working in the store Deborah ran their home, made all their clothes,

Franklin and his illegitimate son William. Deborah Franklin agreed to raise the boy as her own son.

that he couldn't have succeeded in business without her.

There was another part of her marriage that must have been very difficult for Deborah. Before he had become engaged to her, Franklin had had an affair with a woman in Philadelphia. Historians are not certain of the woman's identity but are reasonably sure that she was either a prostitute or a woman of very low status. In his autobiography Franklin wrote, "That hard-to-be-governed passion of youth had hurried me frequently into intrigues with low women that fell in my way."[44] Whoever the woman was she bore a child, a son. Franklin took full responsibility for the baby, whom he named William, and Deborah consented to raise the child as her own.

Poor Richard

and ruined her eyesight spending long hours by candlelight hand-stitching book bindings. Franklin called her "a good and faithful helpmate," and often admitted

It was while running his print shop that Franklin self-published a book that earned him fame and money. Calling it *Poor*

Poor Richard Begins

Poor Richard's Almanack *first made its appearance in December 1732. By the opening words, readers could tell that this almanac would be different from others they had seen.*

"I might in this place attempt to gain thy favor by declaring that I write almanacks with no other view than that of the public good; but in that I should not be sincere, and men are nowadays too wise to be deceived by pretenses, however specious soever. The plain truth of the matter is, I am excessive poor, and my wife, good woman, is, I tell her, excessive proud; she cannot bear, she says, to sit spinning in her shift of tow while I do nothing but gaze at the stars."

Richard's Almanack, he wrote, printed, and sold the book from the time he was twenty-six years old in 1732 until he was fifty-two years old.

There was nothing unique about the idea of publishing an almanac. In fact there were five being published in Philadelphia at the time Franklin decided on *Poor Richard.* Almanacs were important books at the time, and if they were well-done they could earn their publishers quite a bit of money.

Almanacs were popular books—historians say that if a home had but two books, one would be a Bible, the other an almanac. In the eighteenth century almanacs were calendars and tour books, with lists of places where travelers could stay and detailed descriptions of highways and points of interest along the way. Paperbound and pocket size, they "calculated the tides and the changes of the moon, and claimed to forecast the weather. . . . They furnished astrology for those who believed in it. There were sometime recipes . . . and jokes and poems and maxims and odd facts of many sorts."[45]

Poor Richard was a sort of hoax, as were many of Franklin's writings. In his almanac he pretends to be a poor astrologer named Richard Saunders. Saunders writes in the almanac's preface that he was tired of being nagged by his wife to get "a real job" and to stop gazing at stars in order to tell the future.

Franklin also did a couple of things to draw attention to his almanac. First, he promised that besides containing the usual material found in almanacs, *Poor Richard's Almanack* offered advice on both marital problems and those of bachelors.

In addition to this somewhat "racy" material, astrologer Richard Saunders declared the exact date and time of the death of Titan Leeds, Franklin's leading competitor! Of course the predicted day came and went, and Mr. Leeds remained perfectly healthy. But Franklin enjoyed the abundant publicity the stunt aroused in Philadelphia—and the sales of *Poor Richard's Almanack* reflected it.

The title page of Franklin's popular almanac written by him under the pen name Poor Richard. It quickly became a bestseller.

Poor Richard, 1733.
AN
Almanack
For the Year of Chrift
1733,
Being the Firft after LEAP YEAR:

	Years
And makes fince the Creation	
By the Account of the Eastern *Greeks*	7241
By the Latin Church, when ☉ ent. ♈	6932
By the Computation of *W. W.*	5742
By the *Roman* Chronology	5682
By the *Jewish* Rabbies	5494

Wherein is contained

The Lunations, Eclipfes, Judgment of the Weather, Spring Tides, Planets Motions & mutual Afpects, Sun and Moon's Rifing and Setting, Length of Days, Time of High Water, Fairs, Courts, and obfervable Days.

Fitted to the Latitude of Forty Degrees, and a Meridian of Five Hours Weft from *London,* but may without fenfible Error, ferve all the adjacent Places, even from *Newfoundland* to *South-Carolina.*

By *RICHARD SAUNDERS,* Philom.

PHILADELPHIA:
Printed and fold by *B. FRANKLIN,* at the New Printing-Office near the Market.

The Wisdom of Many Ages and Nations

More than ten thousand copies of *Poor Richard* were sold each year, making it a "runaway bestseller," in today's jargon. Each year astrologer Richard Saunders would thank the public for buying his book, saying that his wife had stopped nagging him. He had been able to buy her many new clothes, and she "has been enabled to get a pot of her own, and is no longer obliged to borrow one from a neighbor."[46] The continuing story of Richard Saunders kept the almanac's customers coming back for more each year.

Although the clever publicity stunts were amusing to the almanac's readers, the book was beloved for another reason. Franklin wrote in his autobiography that since most colonists were limited in their education and could not afford books, he thought it a worthwhile purpose to educate them. He did that, he said, by filling "all the little spaces that occurred between the remarkable days of the calendar with proverbial sentences."[47]

Many of these proverbs have survived as well-known sayings, such as "Early to bed and early to rise, makes a man healthy, wealthy, and wise," and "God helps those who help themselves." Franklin compared the little sayings to "scraps from the table of wisdom that will, if well digested, yield strong nourishment to the mind."[48]

Although the words are Franklin's he was the first to point out that the thoughts were borrowed—"the wisdom of many ages and nations." He found proverbs in the writings of poets and philosophers, and even in Bible verses. Sometimes the original sayings were fine as they were, but most of the time Franklin reworked them, making them shorter and clearer. For instance, the old proverb, "Fresh fish and new-come guests smell, but that they are three days old" was streamlined to "Fish and visitors stink in three days."[49]

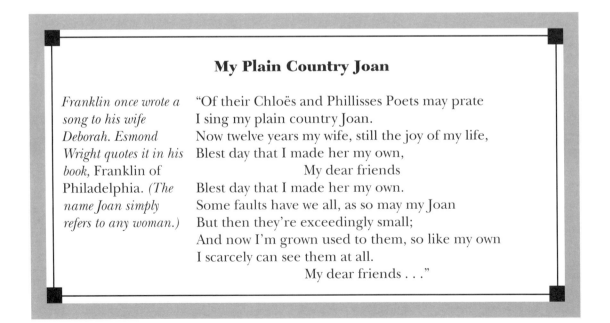

My Plain Country Joan

Franklin once wrote a song to his wife Deborah. Esmond Wright quotes it in his book, Franklin of Philadelphia. *(The name Joan simply refers to any woman.)*

"Of their Chloës and Phillisses Poets may prate
I sing my plain country Joan.
Now twelve years my wife, still the joy of my life,
Blest day that I made her my own,
      My dear friends
Blest day that I made her my own.
Some faults have we all, as so may my Joan
But then they're exceedingly small;
And now I'm grown used to them, so like my own
I scarcely can see them at all.
      My dear friends . . ."

KEEP THY SHOP, AND THY SHOP WILL KEEP THEE.

IF YOU WOULD HAVE YOUR BUSINESS DONE, GO; IF NOT, SEND.

Franklin filled the blank spaces around his almanac entries with proverbs like this one. By doing so, he hoped to instill a little wisdom and moral virtue in his readers, many of whom had little education. Some of the sayings have remained popular to this day.

As the orders for more almanacs poured in, Franklin knew that he had hit upon a successful business venture. Through sales of *Poor Richard* alone he developed his publishing business into the most successful in America. Thousands of copies of the almanac were shipped to Charleston, Boston, Williamsburg, and other cities. Benjamin Franklin, printer, was becoming well known throughout the colonies.

4 From Private Citizen to Public Figure

While a young man in his twenties, Benjamin Franklin's print shop was the focus of his life. He worked fourteen hours a day, and sometimes more, building up his business, finding ways to save money, and expanding the work he did for his clients. Other merchants and business people in Philadelphia were astonished at the energy and long hours he spent in his print shop. "The industry of that Franklin," one merchant stated, "is superior to anything I ever saw of the kind. I see him still at work when I go home . . . and he is at work again before his neighbors are out of bed."[50]

But if that time of his life was focused on private enterprise, Franklin in his thirties was a man with a wider view. Instead of focusing only on his business, he was taking a long look at Philadelphia and seeing how he could help the city prosper, as well.

The Junto

One of the key reasons for this expanded view came from the Junto, a club Franklin had formed in 1727. Its purpose was good

Franklin wheels supplies to the print shop. His neighbors admired him for the long hours and hard work he put in to make his business successful.

Franklin discusses weighty topics with friends and associates outside his print shop. At age twenty (right), Franklin founded the Junto, a formal group that met regularly to debate moral and philosophical questions.

conversation and self-improvement. Historian Esmond Wright called the Junto "part mutual aid society, part social fraternity, part academy."[51]

Franklin had taken the name from the Spanish word *junto,* meaning "together." But it was just as often called the Leather Aprons, for all of its original twelve members were tradesmen—shoemakers, carpenters, clerks, or printers like Franklin himself—who wore such garments when they worked. Like Franklin they were interested in discussing topics such as philosophy, science, and politics.

The Junto met each Friday evening. When the club began, the meetings were held in a tavern; as time went by the Junto rented a room in someone's home for meetings. The members drank wine and put questions to one another for debate.

They addressed such questions as "Can a man arrive at perfection in this life, as some believe; or is it impossible, as others believe?" or, "How shall we judge the goodness of a writing?" or "Which is best to make a friend of, a wise and good man that is poor or a rich man that is neither wise nor good?"

Members of the Junto were required to write essays on a regular basis and present them to the group. Each new member went through a dramatic ceremony in which he had to place his hand over his heart and answer the question, "Do you love truth for truth's sake?"

The Junto thrived for thirty years. During that time other tradesmen wished to become members, and some of the original twelve formed splinter groups. Franklin insisted that the groups never exceed twelve members each, so that conversation could remain intimate. He was extremely proud of the Junto, calling it "the best school of philosophy, morals, and politics that then existed in the province."[52]

The Library Company of Philadelphia

One of the most remarkable things about the Junto was the ideas for projects that came from its members. One such idea was a library—something that did not exist in any city in the colonies. In fact, books were actually rare, prized possessions of those fortunate enough to own them.

There were no stores or shops that exclusively sold books in Philadelphia or anywhere else in America. There were shops that sold a few titles—Franklin's print shop, for example. For the most part those who wanted books sent all the way to England for them.

Franklin proposed that since most of the members owned some books, "it might be convenient to us to have [the books] all together . . . and by clubbing our books to a common library, we should . . . have each of us the advantage of using the books of all the other members, which would be nearly as beneficial as if each owned the whole."[53]

Franklin's idea was met with enthusiasm by the Junto members. A list was put together of other people who might want to contribute books from their personal collections. In addition a list was made of people who had no books to contribute but who were willing to pay a fee for the privilege of using the library.

In all, fifty subscribers paid forty shillings each (equal to about $8.00) to start the library out and promised to pay ten shillings a year after that. The members also drafted a list of brand-new books they wanted to order from England. The books were almost all nonfiction—books about geometry, government, astronomy, and philosophy. The library also had books of Roman and Greek mythology, and a good dictionary.

Franklin and the rest of the Junto members took turns keeping the library at their homes and rotated the job of librarian. Any citizen was welcome to read the books, but only paying members of the subscription library were allowed to check books out.

This was Franklin's first public project, and it was a huge success. The library and its list of subscribers grew, and soon others were copying the idea, starting such libraries in towns all over the colonies.

Fighting Fire with Organization

The success of the subscription library was a great incentive to the Junto, and especially to Franklin. All along he had believed that the public good was an important goal for individual talents. Now he knew that for sure. There were many ways that he and the Junto members could improve the city of Philadelphia.

One of the first needs Franklin recognized was that of a fire department. Fires then were more feared than they are today, for they almost never could be contained. The majority of the buildings and homes were constructed of wood, and once a fire started it kept burning. No

Citizens of Philadelphia use the subscription library. Initiated by Franklin, it was the first lending library in America. It enabled common people to learn about philosophy, religion, history, politics, mathematics, and the sciences. Soon other colonial cities also opened such libraries.

Nineteenth-century artist Charles Washington Wright's depiction of Ben Franklin the fireman. The organized fire departments that are now an institution were originally Franklin's and the Junto's idea.

organization banded people together to fight fires. When a fire started one had to rely on the help of neighbors.

At a Junto meeting in 1736 Franklin proposed that attention should be given to better fire prevention as well as firefighting techniques. The Junto supported him, and Franklin took the matter a step further—to the public.

He wrote a letter to his own paper, the *Gazette*—anonymously, of course. He pretended to be a wise old Philadelphia citizen. In the letter Franklin urged people to take fewer risks with fire. Carrying live coals from room to room, for example, was extremely dangerous, and should only be done if one had a covered container. He also criticized homes with overly narrow hearths and keeping wood near the fireplace

itself. He urged that all chimney sweeps be licensed so that only carefully trained workers could do that important job. His letter also proposed that there be a club in which men could band together to fight fires.

Franklin's scheme worked. He was able to persuade thirty men to join him in forming the Union Fire Company. The members equipped themselves with leather water buckets, along with strong baskets and bags in which valuables from a burning home could be packed and rescued.

The Union Fire Company expanded each year. More and more brigades were organized until, years later, Franklin remarked, "I question whether there is a city in the world better provided with the means of putting a stop to beginning conflagrations."[54]

The City Watch

The city's police system—or lack of one—also troubled Franklin. Each ward had one constable, or police officer, and he, together with a few townspeople chosen each night, walked nightly rounds. If a citizen did not want to take his turn walking rounds, six shillings a year could pay his way out of the job. (The money was supposed to be used to pay substitutes, but as Franklin and most other people knew, the money usually went into the constable's pocket.)

Franklin wrote a paper, which he read at a Junto meeting, that criticized this system. He argued that the constables and their helpers were often sitting in a tavern drinking when they should be out guarding their wards. He also believed that it was unfair to make everyone pay the same six-shilling fee for getting out of city-watch duty. Why should a widow with little property have to pay as much as a wealthy property owner?

He proposed that each citizen pay a tax, the amount to be determined by the value of his or her property. The tax would support a full-time police force. The idea gained popular support and was soon passed by the assembly.

Paving the Streets

Another public project was to pave the streets of Philadelphia. Until the streets were paved they were either covered with a sandy dust that blew into homes and businesses or were a muddy swamp, depending on the weather.

Again Franklin's base of support began with the Junto. They agreed with him that the condition of the streets needed to be improved, and they urged him to take up the issue in the *Gazette*. He wrote letters discussing the benefits of clean, paved streets.

Next, he and a few friends from the Junto paid to have a small section of downtown Philadelphia paved. Franklin hoped that by seeing how much nicer paved streets could be, the townspeople would support the idea for the rest of the city. For his experiment he chose a busy open-market section. In addition to paving the streets with smooth stone, Franklin found someone who, for a small fee, would keep the area swept clear of rubbish on a regular basis.

The effects of the experiment were overwhelming. People saw how clean and attractive the market section of Philadelphia could be with a little maintenance, and they wanted the same for their own streets. They asked Franklin to draw up a detailed proposal for paving the entire city and for taxing the people to pay for it.

Wealth for No Purpose

Although his business thrived Franklin never accumulated money for its own sake. In fact, says historian Thomas Fleming, Franklin believed that one of the greatest vices was "the pursuit of wealth to no purpose."

"[Franklin] liked to tell of the time that a friend showed him through his magnificent new mansion. He took him into a living room large enough to quarter a congress. Franklin asked him why in the world he wanted a room this size. 'Because I can afford it,' said the man. Next came a dining room big enough to seat fifty people. Again Franklin wondered at the size and the man reiterated, 'I can afford it.' Finally, Franklin turned to him and said, 'Why are you wearing such a small hat, why not get one ten times the size of your head? You can afford that, too.'"

A Lesson Learned

Franklin did not stop with these projects. Schools, a hospital, a garbage-removal system—all of these were things Franklin believed would enhance life for the people of his city. Since no one else was doing anything about them, he did. Why did he have such a zeal for public service?

As biographer Carl Van Doren wrote, "He was a man of action, whether in science or morals or politics. He disliked waste and disorder. Pennsylvania, with its mixture of races and its rapid growth and its irregular development, seemed to him disorderly. In that confusion he thought in forms—in forms which life might take."[55]

However, there is a risk to always being the organizer, the one who starts the project. Little jealousies or hurt feelings can make others resentful. One feels, said Franklin, "the impropriety of presenting oneself as the proposer of any useful project that might be supposed to raise one's reputation in the smallest degree above that of one's neighbors."

Franklin could have seemed a nuisance to some in Philadelphia. However, he learned early on that it was a good idea to keep both his name and his face out of the public eye. Sometimes he would tell people that the idea he promoted was not his, but rather a friend's. Things went more smoothly, he later said, when he realized that he didn't need to claim credit for everything he did. The truth about who deserved credit would eventually be known. He wrote, "The present little sacrifice [to my] vanity will afterwards be amply repaid."[56]

To Public Office

Even though he tried to keep himself out of the public eye, people were aware that

---

Advertising in the *Gazette*

Franklin's Pennsylvania Gazette *was a mirror of the people in the early 1700s. His newspaper gave no evidence that Franklin objected to the buying and selling of slaves, as this excerpt from the May 2, 1733, issue shows:*

"[Advertisement:] There is to be sold a very likely Negro woman aged about 30 years who has lived in this city, from her childhood, and can wash and iron very well, cook victuals, sew, spin on the linen wheel, milk cows, and do all sorts of housework very well. She has a boy of about two years old, which is to go with her. The price is reasonable as you can agree.

And also another very likely boy aged about six years, who is son of the above said woman. He will be sold with his mother, or by himself, as the buyer pleases. Enquire of the Printer."

Franklin was a key figure in the public affairs of Philadelphia. For that reason he was elected clerk of the Pennsylvania General Assembly in 1736.

Being part of the colony's legislative body was an honor, but Franklin found it boring most of the time. He thought the long speeches dull and believed that the assembly's work could be done in less than half the time if its representatives would get to the point more quickly.

Even though Franklin would rather have been working on his newspaper or some other project while the assembly was meeting, there were definite advantages to being part of it. For one thing, he met a number of new people, many of whom were influential members of the community. Together with Franklin's friends from the Junto, the assembly members gave him a wide base of support for future projects in the city.

The clerk position was good for Franklin's printing business, too. The work of the assembly generated lots of paper work—votes and laws needed to be printed, as well as the paper money needed by the colony. Because of his ties to the assembly Franklin was able to land nearly all of these printing jobs himself.

The same was true for another public service post he accepted the following year—that of deputy postmaster of Philadelphia. It was a part-time job and it did not interfere with his printing business. The post office was set up next door to his print shop and store.

Both he and Deborah Franklin worked hard at the postmaster job. She found it exciting to be the first in town to hear news from overseas. And Franklin himself was pleased because as postmaster he did not have to pay postage for the *Gazette*.

With the money he saved in postage he was able to build up the newspaper's circulation.

Taking a Stand

Most of Franklin's ideas were accepted by everyone. There was one instance in 1747, however, in which he took a stand that guaranteed a stir. It had to do with Pennsylvania's military defenses.

The colony had no defense system. There was no standing army, no militia, no fortresses where settlers could go in case of emergency, no artillery or other supplies. If attacked, the colony was almost helpless.

The reason for Pennsylvania's lack of defense against attacks was that it was founded as a Quaker colony. The Quakers are a religious sect that strongly oppose war and fighting of any kind. And since they would never fight, why would they need weapons and soldiers?

The majority of delegates to the Pennsylvania General Assembly were Quakers, and they refused to spend tax money on defense. They had a well-earned reputation of pacifism and were not interested in changing their ways. As one historian writes, "[The Quakers] had no quarrel with Spain or France, and they had always been at peace with the Indians. Let men who started wars finish them."[57]

In a very real sense Pennsylvania—or any other American colony—had the same enemies that England had. Spain had been England's enemy since 1739. And in 1744 England and France began fighting, but their battles were mostly confined to the European continent.

Even so, the news of England's wars with Spain and France caused nervous whispers among some colonists. What if those nations decided to strike at England by attacking her American colonies? What if France used its influence with some of the native American tribes and set them against the colonists?

In July 1747 the fear became reality. French and Spanish privateers, pirates hired by those governments, approached the American coast. They captured a British ship nearby and murdered its captain and crew. The privateers then sailed up the Delaware River and burned and looted two large Pennsylvania farms. Pennsylvania became caught up in violence aimed at England.

Plain Truth

Franklin made his move. He petitioned wealthy merchants and business people who were not Quakers. Wouldn't they be eager to put up money to defend their homes and businesses?

Not, as it turned out, if it meant protecting the Quakers, too. The merchants felt it was unfair for their money to be used to protect people who refused to help fight off the attackers. And without the leadership of the assembly and the money of the wealthy Pennsylvanians, any hope of a defense was certainly dim.

Franklin rushed to press with his *Gazette,* explaining the problem to the average citizen. As the days went by and more people talked about the issue, he put out a pamphlet called *Plain Truth; or, Serious Considerations on the Present State of the City of Philadelphia and Province of Pennsylvania by a Tradesman of Philadelphia.*

The pamphlet criticized both the Quakers for their refusal to raise an army and the obstinance of the wealthy merchants. "Till of late," Franklin wrote in *Plain Truth,* "I could scarce believe the story of him who refused to pump in a sinking ship because one on board whom he hated would be saved by it as well as himself."[58]

The pamphlet appealed to Pennsylvanians to forget their pride and their petty grievances and to pull together. He reminded them of the incredible power of people to do things themselves. Franklin urged them to come to a town meeting and start an army.

The number of people responding, expected to be around a thousand, turned into more than ten thousand. Men organized themselves into bands. They armed themselves and began training and drilling. Franklin organized a lottery to raise money to purchase cannons and other military supplies.

It was not only the men of Pennsylvania who rose to the call. "The women," Franklin wrote in his autobiography, "by subscriptions among themselves, provided silk colors which they presented to the companies, painted with different devices and mottoes which I supplied."[59]

The beginnings of the Revolutionary War were still decades away, but the spirit of independence was very much alive in Pennsylvania. Since the governmental powers in the colony refused to get involved, common people found they could accomplish a great deal on their own. Although the military threat posed by the French and Spanish privateers never amounted to very much, the lesson learned by Franklin and his fellow colonists would prove to be invaluable within the next twenty-five years.

Chapter

5 The Scientist and Inventor

In 1748, at the age of forty-two, Benjamin Franklin had become weary of business. He had enjoyed the challenge of making money, but to continue to make money for its own sake was no longer appealing.

He was, by standards of the time, a wealthy man. Clerks in Philadelphia made twenty-five pounds each year, teachers at the academy made between sixty and seventy pounds, and Pennsylvania's governor made one thousand. Franklin's yearly income from his print shop and the *Gazette* was over five thousand pounds. He owned several houses and collected rent on them, in addition to his small salary as deputy postmaster.

In 1748 Franklin made the decision to retire. Most men of the time who decided to stop working at a trade or business did so with the idea of resting and enjoying their last years. But Franklin—quite unknown to him—was only halfway through his life and had quite a different view of how to spend it.

The Natural Philosopher

What interested Franklin now was science. It was not called science in those days, but "natural philosophy." Included in natural philosophy were the study of mathematics, physics, geography, biology, and chemistry, among other disciplines. There were no scientists then, either—merely people who were wealthy enough to have the time to dabble in such pursuits.

Franklin had always been interested in such things. He had an active, questioning mind, even as a boy. His experiments with faster ways of swimming had been evidence of that. He enjoyed looking at a phenomenon—whether it was the behavior of ants, or a current running through a river—and trying to understand it.

Natural philosophy was an exciting pursuit in the eighteenth century, especially in Europe. In England the Royal Society was a committed organization of philosophers who enjoyed sharing their findings with one another. The society had regular meetings at which new scientific discoveries were discussed.

But nothing like that was happening in America. Those who enjoyed natural philosophy worked alone. There were no large laboratories or scientific societies to support or encourage them. Five years before his retirement Franklin had access to many newspapers because of his job as deputy postmaster, and he read with great interest of the discoveries happening in other cities. He had, as one biographer puts it, "an impulse to bring them some-how together, as he had brought the members of the Junto when he was a journeyman [trained worker]." [60]

The association he proposed then was to be an American version of the Royal Society. Called the American Philosophical Society, it was to be based in Philadelphia. It would meet monthly, and its members, like those of the Royal Society, would pool whatever findings they had with the group. Franklin offered his services as secretary and later served as president.

A few of Franklin's old Junto friends formed the backbone of the original society. The organization got off to a slow start. Its meetings were erratic, and its members were less active in their scientific pursuits than Franklin would have liked. In a letter to a friend he complained, "The members . . . here are very idle gentlemen. They will take no pains." [61]

But gradually the society grew and became more productive. Papers on interesting subjects such as gravity and inertia were presented, and Franklin became more satisfied. And as with many of Franklin's projects, the American Philosophical Society has lived on, evolving into a highly respected association still active today.

Blue Sparks and Magic Jars

Although Franklin was interested in almost every aspect of natural philosophy, one area fascinated him more than all others—electricity. Very little was understood about electricity in the mid-1700s, but what Franklin had seen captivated him.

A few years before his retirement he had been visiting in Boston. There he had

EXPERIMENTS

AND

OBSERVATIONS

ON

ELECTRICITY,

MADE AT

Philadelphia in *America*,

BY

Mr. BENJAMIN FRANKLIN,

AND

Communicated in several Letters to Mr. P. COLLINSON of *London*, F. R. S.

_____

LONDON:

Printed and sold by E. CAVE, at *St. John's Gate.* 1751.
(Price 2s. 6d.)

Franklin wrote about his electrical experiments to Peter Collinson, his friend in London's Royal Society. Collinson had some of Franklin's findings published. This title page belonged to one such publication.

met Dr. Archibald Spencer, a scientist from Scotland. Spencer had a sort of traveling lecture during which he did "tricks" with static electricity. The most remarkable of these was suspending a little boy from the ceiling by silk threads and drawing sparks from the boy's ears, hands, and feet!

Such stunts amazed his audience and probably frightened them as well. Educated people thought it was a mysterious force; others believed it was magic.

Some scientists had found that they could produce electricity by rubbing glass tubes with silk. The rubbing produced what was often referred to as "electrical fire." In Europe scientists had proved that this electrical fire could be transmitted through some things, such as metal, but not through other things, such as wood.

A breakthrough in the study of electricity occurred in 1746 at the University of Leyden, in the Netherlands. A scientist named Pieter van Musschenbroek invented what was actually the first condenser, a way to store electricity. It was a glass jar covered with tinfoil. The jar was filled with water and had a cork stopper. A wire was stuck through the cork into the jar, and static electricity transmitted through the wire into the jar would remain there. If one touched the wire of a Leyden jar, one received a jolt from the stored electricity.

The Leyden jar eventually proved to be an important scientific tool. At first, however, it was as mysterious as the electrical fire it stored. People like Archibald Spencer based their traveling shows on tricks that could be performed using the jar, such as pulling sparks from the little boy.

Little Leisure for Anything Else

Franklin found Spencer's demonstrations in Boston enthralling. He persuaded the scientist to come to Philadelphia. After performing more of his tricks there, Spencer sold his equipment to an excited Franklin.

To the Leyden jars and other things he got from Spencer, Franklin added more equipment. He wrote to his friend Peter Collinson, a member of the Royal Society in England, and asked him to send whatever he could.

Early tools used in the study of electricity include Leyden jars (left) and a glass tube (right), which, when rubbed with silk, produced a static electric charge.

The months that followed were devoted to the study of electricity. He found that this branch of science engrossed him like no other. In a letter to Collinson in 1747 Franklin wrote,

> I never was before engaged in any study that so totally engrossed my attention and my time as this has lately done, for what with making experiments when I can be alone, and repeating them to my friends and acquaintances who, from the novelty of the thing, come continually in crowds to see them, I have during some months past had little leisure time for anything else.[62]

These devices were designed by Ben Franklin for use in his experiments with electricity. When he couldn't get special equipment, his inventiveness enabled him to use common household items to conduct his experiments.

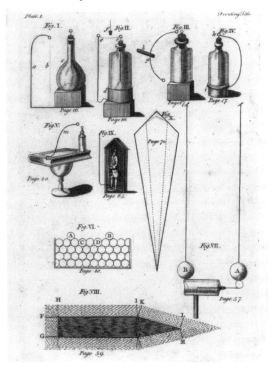

He soon tired of merely repeating others' experiments and set to work on some of his own. As usual, Franklin was eager to understand what made things work and was able to answer questions that other researchers in the new field of electronics had not even asked yet. He explained, for instance, what it was about the Leyden jar that stored electricity. He discovered the existence of positive and negative charges. And it was Franklin who was responsible for much of the vocabulary of electricity—condenser, conductor, battery, and electric shock.

Franklin utilized what equipment he could purchase from Collinson and other sources, but he was not limited to it. He started his experiments with modern equipment but also used such common materials as a salt cellar, a vinegar cruet, a pump handle, and gold used on the binding of a book. One early writer said that Franklin "could make an experiment with less apparatus and conduct his experimental inquiry to a discovery with more ordinary materials than any other philosopher we ever saw."[63]

Dancing Spiders and Golden Crowns

Although Franklin was serious about his studies, he used electricity to have a great deal of fun. He entertained friends with a "spider" made of a piece of burnt cork and linen threads, which he charged with an electric current. The electricity made the artificial spider dance "in a very entertaining manner, appearing perfectly alive to persons unacquainted."

Another of Franklin's tricks involved a portrait of King George II. Franklin added a fine layer of gold to the inside of the painting's frame so that it would conduct an electric current. He used the same gold to fashion a crown on the king's head.

Franklin would ask someone to hold the painting and at the same time try to remove King George's crown. If the person were touching the crown and the frame simultaneously, there would be a loud cracking sound, and the unwary volunteer would receive a terrible shock.

Franklin could remove the crown without harm as long as he took care to avoid touching the gold on the frame. This, he said, proved that he was loyal to the king, while the other person clearly was not. In fact, Franklin wrote, "If the picture were highly charged, the consequence might perhaps be as fatal as that of high-treason."[64]

Cooking a Turkey, Almost Killing a Goose

Aside from doing such tricks Franklin was most interested in how electricity might be put to practical use. He once proposed a whole banquet prepared by use of electricity.

This "party of pleasure," as he termed it, would be held on the banks of the Schuylkill River. It would begin with a turkey or goose killed by an electric shock and roasted on an "electric jack" over a fire that would be lighted by an electrically charged bottle. The guests' glasses of brandy would be lit by means of a spark sent over the river, using the water as a conductor. There would also be little glasses of wine that would be electrified, giving off a tiny shock as they were brought to the lips. As the partygoers offered toasts to the health of all the famous European electricians, guns would be fired—by an electrical charge, of course.

Historians do not agree on whether such a banquet ever took place. However, it is known that Franklin used electricity to kill turkeys and other birds. He thought it a more humane way of killing animals. He also claimed that birds killed by lightning strikes were more tender than those killed in more traditional ways.

In one demonstration of this Franklin almost killed himself. He had charged two Leyden jars, which held many times more electrical charge than usual. Not paying complete attention to what he was doing, he touched both wires at the same time, taking the electricity into his body.

Franklin could not remember what happened next, for the jolt of electricity knocked him unconscious for a moment. But others who were present told him later that there was a great flash, and also a cracking sound as loud as a pistol. "I neither saw the one nor heard the other," wrote Franklin, "nor did I feel the stroke of my hand. . . . I then felt what I know not well how to describe: a universal blow throughout my whole body from head to foot."[65]

Franklin made light of the incident, although it could easily have resulted in his death. "I meant to cook a turkey," he joked to his guests, "but it seems I almost killed a goose!"[66]

An Idea About Lightning

Franklin, with his usual interest in detail, kept methodical accounts of each electrical experiment he performed. He published

Works of the Devil

Some people, as historian Thomas Fleming writes, feared that by tampering with lightning, Franklin was going against God's will.

"Inevitably, there was some opposition from those who made it a business to superintend the relationship between men and God. When an earthquake struck Boston in 1755, one preacher assured his congregation that it was a warning from on high, because so many in the city were defying the divine will by resorting to those works of the devil, lightning rods."

no formal scientific papers, as European scientists did. Instead he wrote letters regularly to his friend in London, Peter Collinson. In these letters, which Collinson shared with his colleagues, Franklin simply and clearly laid out the results of each new finding.

Many of these were so interesting that Collinson read them aloud at meetings of the Royal Society. The most interesting of Franklin's letters about experiments were translated into several languages, including Latin, the language of science in the eighteenth century. The work for which Franklin became most famous had to do with lightning.

In the eighteenth century lightning was a terrifying, mysterious force to most people. One common belief was that lightning was caused by demons. Church bells were thought to have magic powers to drive away such demons; in fact, many bells had inscriptions claiming their power to ward off evil lightning strikes.

Franklin believed that lightning was electricity—a notion that he was not the first to propose. However, it was he who first found a way of proving that the two were one and the same.

He proposed that a man climb to the top of a very tall platform when a storm approached. The platform should be insulated, because a long iron rod was to pierce it, twenty or thirty feet into the air. The idea, Franklin said, was that the iron rod—a conductor—would draw the electricity from the storm clouds to the man standing on the platform. If Franklin's theory were correct the electricity from the clouds would transfer to the man, who "might be electrified and afford sparks."[67]

An International Celebrity

Franklin proposed the experiment in 1750. He wanted to be the first to try it, but there was a stumbling block. Nowhere in Philadelphia was there a building or hill high enough for an iron rod to scrape storm clouds. Christ Church had not yet been built; Franklin was waiting until its completion to try his experiment.

A French scientist named D'Alibard beat him to it. D'Alibard had read about Franklin's theory and set out to test it in

1751, on the hilly outskirts of Paris. He set up a forty-foot iron rod on a wooden platform. When lightning struck the rod, an assistant ran to the base of the rod and touched it with a Leyden jar. The bluish-white glow of electricity being conducted from the rod to the jar was proof that Franklin had been correct.

In the instant that lightning hit the metal rod, Franklin became famous. By removing the cloak of mystery from lightning he earned worldwide praise. The king of France sent him a special commendation. Scientists throughout Europe hailed him as a genius, or "virtuoso"—a word used then for a particularly brilliant scientist. All of a sudden a retired printer whose hobby was science had become an international celebrity.

However, the scientific achievement for which Franklin has become legendary in America is his experiment with the kite in a thunderstorm. Countless pictures and stories of Franklin and his kite have underscored its importance to the world of science. Interestingly, historians are not certain whether the experiment ever really took place!

The Kite

Franklin never wrote a firsthand account of flying a kite in Philadelphia. The only record historians have is that of a friend of Franklin's named Joseph Priestly. Priestly wrote that in 1752, about six months after D'Alibard's experiment in Paris, Franklin performed an experiment testing his own theory. (Franklin had not yet received word of the French scientist's success.)

In one of the most well known stories about Franklin, he uses a kite and a key to determine if lightning was electricity. Historians are uncertain if the experiment really took place.

Priestly wrote that Franklin and his son William (then twenty-one years old) constructed a kite out of a silk handkerchief and wooden slats. To the top of the kite Franklin fastened a sharp, pointed wire. This would perform like the iron rod of his previously suggested experiment. The kite was necessary, of course, because no tall building was available in Philadelphia.

Franklin tied a metal key to the end of a long silk ribbon at the base of the kite. Franklin hoped that if electricity was in the storm clouds, as he suspected, the charge would go from the metal wire down the string to the key.

But there was no immediate result. As Priestly wrote, "The kite being raised, a considerable time elapsed before there was any appearance of its being electrified. One very promising cloud had passed over it without any effect." Finally, "just as [Franklin] was beginning to despair of his contrivance," he noticed some of the threads of the string standing straight up, as though electrified. He touched the key carefully with his knuckle and "perceived a very evident electric spark."[68]

If the experiment did take place it did no more than confirm what D'Alibard had already proven—that Franklin had been absolutely correct in his theory.

Applying Science

Once he knew for certain that he was correct about lightning, Franklin set to work finding a practical use for his knowledge. For him it did not seem enough just to know that lightning was electricity. How could that knowledge help people?

Thunderstorms were greatly feared in the eighteenth century, for the lightning that accompanied them quite often struck houses and barns, burning them to the ground. But Franklin found that buildings could be made safe by attaching tall metal rods atop them. Attached to the rod was a wire that led down the outside of the building and into the ground. The lightning

---

This Field Has Been Plastered

Franklin believed that plaster should be used as a fertilizer. As Frank Donovan quotes in The Benjamin Franklin Papers, *Franklin had an unusual way of proving it.*

"As an object lesson to other farmers, [Franklin] wrote with plaster in a field along the highway, THIS FIELD HAS BEEN PLASTERED. The white letters soon disappeared, but when the crop came up, the message reappeared in the greener, more lush growth of the fertilized letters."

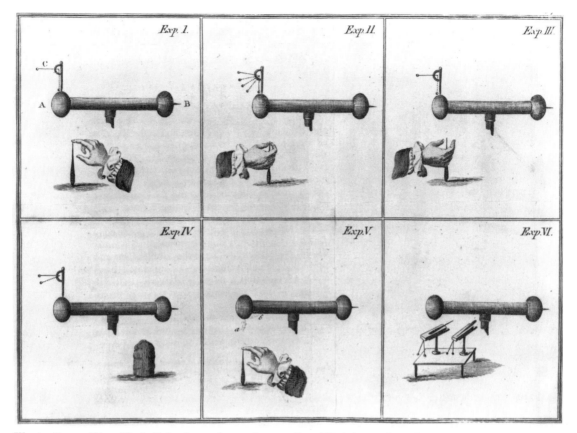

Illustrations of Franklin's lightning rod experiments. Franklin's invention of the lightning rod, which discharges lightning's destructive electricity safely into the ground, won him worldwide fame and respect.

would hit the rod and carry the great electrical charge harmlessly into the ground.

This practical application of science was met with as much excitement as Franklin's earlier theory. Lightning rods were erected on steeples of churches, on towers, houses high on hills—even on the masts of ships. And from cities and towns around the world came letters of praise and thanks to the scientist who had lessened lightning's terrible threat.

The name of Benjamin Franklin became widely known in literature, too. Essayists wrote heroic accounts of Franklin's work. Irish immigrant Thomas Campbell, in his poem "Pleasures of Hope," wrote about people who would "with Franklin grasp the lightning's fiery wing."[69] And an American poet, Gordon Forrest, wrote:

> Some write in blood a name
> Which fame is ever brightening;
> But Franklin had a heavenly air
> And wrote his name with lightning.[70]

The First of Many

The lightning rod, or Franklin rod as it was called for years, was one of many inventions

Franklin documents his invention of bifocals. The glasses allow the wearer to clearly see objects both near and far. This invention, like most of Franklin's, was intended to improve people's lives.

for which Franklin was responsible. Behind almost all of these inventions was a desire to make some task easier, to find a way to improve things.

For instance, Franklin invented bifocals because he found ordinary glasses were not always useful. Sometimes he needed help seeing close objects, while other times he had trouble focusing on things farther away. He had two pairs of glasses and found switching back and forth to be terribly annoying.

He asked a glass cutter to cut apart the lenses of both pairs of glasses. Franklin then glued the bottoms of one set of lenses to the tops of the other. He found the new glasses "more particularly convenient since . . . the glasses that serve me best at table to see what I eat not being the best to see the faces of those on the other side of the table who speak to me."[71]

Franklin also invented the first odometer, a device that could be attached to the axle of a wagon wheel and give an approximate measure of the vehicle's mileage. He devised a mechanical extending arm, useful for taking books off high library shelves. It was he who first proposed a system of daylight savings time. Franklin made the first rocking chair and invented what is known today as a "school chair," a wooden chair with an attached desk for an arm.

His genius for inventing even crossed the line into the realm of music. He created a new instrument called an "armonica." It was made of thirty-seven glass hemispheres that could be turned with a foot pedal. The armonica player would

"'Tis the Wreck of a World We Live On!"

One of Franklin's remarkable observations included his belief that the earth was once completely covered by water.

"'Now I mention mountains,' he wrote to his friend Jared Eliot in 1747, 'it occurs [to me] to tell you that the great Appalachian Mountains, which run from York River back of these Colonies to the Bay of Mexico, show in many places near the highest part of them, strata of sea shells, in some places the marks of them are in the solid rocks. 'Tis certainly the *wreck* of a world we live on!'"

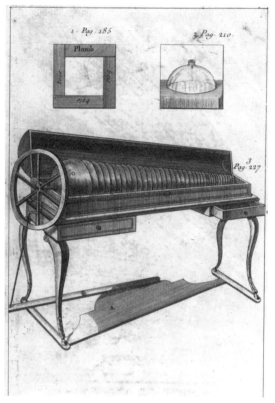

The rotating glass hemispheres of Franklin's armonica produced clear, bell-like tones. Both Mozart and Beethoven composed works for it.

press against the rotating hemispheres with moistened fingers, thus producing a clear, bell-like tone. The armonica was popular for forty years, and both Beethoven and Mozart composed pieces for it.

Efficient Heat

The Franklin stove is the invention for which he is best known. It was designed as an improvement over the standard fireplace. In Franklin's day fireplaces were used as a home's primary source of heat. But sitting directly next to the fireplace, one roasted, while sitting several feet away, one froze. Too little of the heat came into the room; most went up the chimney.

As Franklin later wrote, such extremes of hot and cold were unhealthy: "Women . . . (as they sit much in the house) get colds in the head, rheums, and defluxions, which fall into their jaws and gums, and have destroyed many a fine set of teeth in these

The Franklin stove heated rooms much more efficiently than a traditional fireplace did. The stove was used in homes for more than a century.

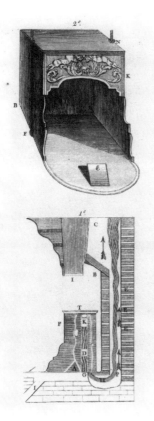

A diagram of how a Franklin stove works. The metal firebox (top) radiates heat from the fire within it out into the room. Vents draw smoke up the chimney (bottom) without letting heat escape.

northern colonies. Great and bright fires also do very much to contribute to damage the eyes, dry and shrivel the skin, and bring on early the appearance of old age."[72]

To solve all of these problems Franklin devised a boxlike structure made of iron that fit into an existing fireplace. As the iron sides of the structure became hot, the heat radiated forward into the room, rather than up the chimney.

It was a simple idea, but it worked extremely well. In time Franklin perfected it, adding grates, heating panels, and sliding doors. And the Franklin stove, or Pennsylvania stove as it was sometimes called, was used in homes for more than a century.

Franklin could have become rich from any one of these inventions. The state assembly of Pennsylvania even offered him a patent for the Franklin stove, but he refused. And his 1753 edition of *Poor Richard* contained free advice on how to make and install lightning rods in the essay "How to Secure Houses etc. from Lightning."

As historian Esmond Wright says, "Through all of [Franklin's] scientific correspondence, he clearly saw himself as a member of an international team of inquirers and experimenters, living by the free interchange of information. His attitude was open and generous, ceaselessly questing, and devoid of vanity."[73]

Unfortunately for the world of science a new pursuit was to take Franklin away from his inventions. An age of political struggle was approaching, and he soon would become a key player.

6 Thinking Continentally

Franklin had been a clerk in Pennsylvania's General Assembly since 1736. In 1748 he was elected as a regular member of the assembly, a position with far more responsibility and prestige.

More importantly to Franklin, the position would be more interesting. As clerk he had spent much of his time looking out a window, or doing Magic Squares, a kind of mathematical puzzle. In 1744 he had written to his friend in London, William Strahan: "We have seldom any news on our side of the globe that can be interesting to you. . . . All our affairs are *petit* [small]."[74]

The Deputy Postmaster

Once elected Franklin was instantly a leader in the assembly. He rarely gave speeches, for he always felt he spoke

An Embarrassing Incident

In 1756 the officers of the Philadelphia regiment voted Franklin their colonel. In his autobiography Franklin recalls that the same regiment embarrassed him by giving him a military escort when he left on postal business for Virginia.

"Just as I was getting on horseback they came to my door, between thirty and forty, mounted and all in their uniforms. I had not been previously acquainted with the project, or I should have prevented it . . . and I was a good deal chagrined at their appearance, as I could not avoid their accompanying me. What made it worse was that, as soon as we began to move, they drew their swords and rode with them naked all the way.

Somebody wrote an account of this to the proprietor [of the colony, Thomas Penn], and it gave him great offense. No such honor had been paid him when in the province, or to any of his governors."

In Franklin's day, mail and people were carried between cities by stagecoach (right). For shorter distances or to places not having stagecoach service, mail was carried by an individual on horseback (left).

poorly. But he had a genius for getting things done behind the scenes. As biographer Van Doren writes, "shaping opinions, harmonizing differences, and . . . summing up in incomparable and irresistible statements."[75]

Besides being an assemblyman in Philadelphia, Franklin had his sights set on another position. He learned that the deputy postmaster general for the American colonies had died. Franklin wanted the job and set out to get it. The position involved more responsibility than his current post, for he would be responsible not just for Philadelphia's postal system, but for those of all the American colonies.

He wrote to his old friend from the Royal Society, Peter Collinson, to use whatever influence he had to get Franklin the job. He sent three hundred pounds to cover whatever fees or charges Collinson might be faced with.

Collinson was able to get Franklin one-half of the position. The government in London decided to split the job between Franklin and a man named William Hunter. Hunter, like Franklin, was a printer, who published a newspaper in his home colony of Virginia. As it turned out Hunter became chronically ill, so most of the work was left to Franklin.

Historians are quick to point out that in pursuing the position, Franklin violated one of his own rules—never seek public office. Franklin had always thought it unbecoming to compete for a job. This particular position, however, had too many advantages to pass up.

For one thing, to be deputy postmaster was a high honor for the colony. The position would mean that Philadelphia would be the center of the colonial postal system—a great amount of prestige for that city. And Franklin would be able to travel throughout the colonies on a government expense account.

When he took over the position Franklin was quick to share his good fortune; he placed his relatives in key jobs with the postal service. His son William became the comptroller (supervisor of accounts) of all of the northern colonies' post offices. His brother John became postmaster of Boston; brother Peter took charge of Franklin's former job as the postmaster of Philadelphia.

What a change Franklin made in the postal system! He shaved the time it took for a letter to get from Boston to Philadelphia from six weeks to three. He took advantage of the travel allowance and personally visited the various colonies under his domain. He noted roads in ill repair, broken bridges, or anything else that might slow a mail rider. He used this information to streamline the postal routes. He even saw to it that milestones along those routes were erected to give riders an opportunity to pace themselves.

He changed the rules so that all newspapers had to pay postage—even his own *Gazette*. He straightened out the accounting system. He even originated the "penny post," a system that charged an extra penny for home delivery to people who didn't go to the post office to collect their mail. Within months the postal service, which had never made money since its beginnings, was turning a nice profit.

The Albany Congress

While Franklin worked hard to make an efficient postal system, bigger events were underway in the colonies. In 1754 the on-again, off-again hostilities between France and England flared into war, and the war spilled over into the American colonies. There was danger in Pennsylvania.

The French in North America had strongholds in Canada and as far west as the Allegheny River, at the eastern end of the Ohio River Valley. Fearing the loss of their profitable fur trade there, the French were building forts and military outposts, getting ready to do battle with the English settlers. Too, the French settlers were using their influence to encourage some native American tribes to carry out brutal attacks on the English settlers. The British government was so worried about the French and Indian aggression, in fact, that they urged representatives from each of the colonies to have a meeting to decide what should be done.

The meeting was held in Albany, New York, and included representatives from seven of the American colonies. Since they had no history of working together, the colonies were at a disadvantage against the French. As one of the delegates to the Albany Congress, Franklin wanted to lay out his plan for strengthening and uniting the colonies.

His plan was based on a native American union he had seen years before in western Pennsylvania. There were six different tribes in the area, but they had organized themselves into one large association, known as the Six Nations of the Iroquois. As an assembly delegate Franklin had had occasion to deal with the Six Nations.

Like most Europeans he had trouble understanding native American culture. To Franklin and others the natives were frightening savages—far below the sophistication of "refined," white Europeans. But the more he learned about the Six Nations, the more Franklin admired the strength and security they had created by their union. He wrote,

> It would be a strange thing if six nations of ignorant savages should be capable of forming a scheme for such a union, and be able to execute it in such a manner that it has subsisted ages . . . and yet that a like union should be impractical for ten or a dozen English colonies to whom it is more necessary.[76]

The plan Franklin proposed in Albany called for one general government—the first time such a federal idea had ever been proposed in America. The government would be composed of all the colonies, said Franklin, but "within and under which government each colony may retain its present constitution."[77]

Such a federal government would be helpful in organizing defenses in war time and in making improvements for the common good during times of peace. It could be funded, Franklin suggested, by a tax on liquor, on pubs (bars), or on tea.

No Thoughts of Rebellion

It is important to understand that at this time there was nothing in Franklin's plan that called for independence from England. Franklin and the other colonists considered themselves loyal subjects of the Crown, and they did not want to change that. On the contrary, says historian Catherine Drinker Bowen, "what they desired was protection from the French. They wanted British troops sent over; they wanted the Crown—not the colonies—to pay for the erection of forts along the frontier. Rebellion does not sit well with a yearning for maternal shelter."[78]

Franklin's plan was met with suspicion. The smaller colonies worried that in a union of states they might be swallowed up by larger ones. The larger colonies were reluctant to give up even a little of their power.

The Albany Congress did finally hammer out a plan for a union, and the delegates agreed to take it back to their

A meeting of leaders of the Six Nations of the Iroquois. The Indian organization inspired Ben Franklin to suggest a similar confederacy for the American colonies.

individual assemblies to vote on it. In addition, the proposal was sent to Parliament in London, for its approval. However, neither the colonies nor the British government accepted Franklin's plan.

The colonies could not overcome their jealousies and suspicions, while Parliament felt the plan was too radical. The plan was rejected, and Franklin was disgusted. "Everybody cries, a Union is absolutely necessary," he wrote to a friend, "but when they come to the manner and form of their Union, their weak noddles are presently distracted."[79]

Franklin graphically expressed his opinion on the need to unite the colonies with this drawing of a disjointed snake. In doing so, he published the first American political cartoon.

Join or Die

Even after his plan was defeated Franklin continued trying to present it in different ways. He rewrote parts of the plan and asked friends to read and comment on it. He talked about his union plan in the *Gazette,* too, and in 1754 came up with the first political cartoon ever printed to support his idea.

It was very simple—a sketch of a snake broken into eight segments. Each segment was labeled with the name of a colony: New England, New York, New Jersey, Pennsylvania, Maryland, Virginia, North Carolina, and South Carolina. The headline read, "Join or Die."

Representation in Parliament

Franklin objected to governor William Shirley's proposals for union in a series of letters in 1754. This excerpt is taken from Andrew Allison's book, The Real Benjamin Franklin.

"The people . . . will say, and perhaps with justice that . . . to propose taxing them by Parliament, and refuse them the liberty of choosing a representative council to meet in the colonies and consider and judge of the necessity of any general tax, and the [amount], shows suspicion of their loyalty to the Crown, or of their regard for their country, or of their common sense and understanding, which they have not deserved."

Although Franklin was adamant about the need for union, he was just as adamant in his insistence that he was a loyal British subject. Even so, he had no hesitation about speaking out against what he felt was stupidity or foolishness in Britain's actions toward the colonies. For instance, the British government had a policy of sending English convicts to the colonies under the guise of "the improvement and well-peopling of the colonies."

Writing under the name Americanus in the *Gazette,* Franklin suggested sending a return gift to England to thank them for their interest and concern about the colonies. Rattlesnakes, he wrote, could be caught in America and sent to England. Thousands of the "venomous reptiles" could be set loose throughout the country, "but particularly in the gardens of the prime ministers, the lords of trade, and members of Parliament, for to them we are most particularly obliged."[80]

Danger on the Frontier

In his life Franklin achieved fame as many things—inventor, scientist, statesman—but not as a military hero. His only military service occurred during the French and Indian War, not long after the Albany Congress.

The French and their native allies had stepped up their raids on English settlements and towns along the frontier. In November 1756 the little village of Gnadenhuetten, along the northern frontier of Pennsylvania, was attacked. Many of

A painting of the Battle of Monongahela during the French and Indian War. Franklin's only military service came during this war, which pitted the French and their native American allies against the British colonists.

its inhabitants, mostly German immigrants, were killed, and the village burned to the ground.

Franklin, along with two other members of the assembly, was sent to Gnadenhuetten to arrange for and build defenses in the area. Franklin and his colleagues had two hundred men in their command, and although he had no military rank, the settlers along the frontier called him general.

Having nothing but an old book to guide them, Franklin and his troops built forts and stockades until the area was once again secure. In sleet and cold, sleeping in a tent and drafty barn, Franklin celebrated his fiftieth birthday.

In a letter to his wife back in Philadelphia, who occasionally sent food to them, Franklin joked that he was enjoying the life of a soldier. "Your citizens that have their dinners hot . . . know nothing of good eating. We find it in much greater perfection when the kitchen is fourscore miles from the dining room."[81]

Colonel Franklin

After his mission was completed Franklin returned to Philadelphia, only to find that local supporters had pressured the royal governor into appointing him colonel of the Philadelphia regiment. Franklin was greatly surprised, and not completely happy about it, since he knew next to nothing about military matters.

The rank of colonel turned out to be somewhat of a nuisance, too. He was given a military escort back to his home, and out of respect for their leader, soldiers fired their guns in a salute outside his door. The explosion knocked over shelves in his workroom, smashing Leyden jars and other glass devices.

Franklin had bought the equipment as a pastime to fill up his retirement years. Although he had more than thirty years of life remaining, he would never have the time for his experiments again.

7 Making Enemies

As the war with the French and the Indians continued, the Pennsylvania assembly continued to raise taxes to pay for the defense of the colony. Farmers paid taxes on the property they owned, but such taxes could not possibly pay for the huge defense bills. Unfortunately for the General Assembly, the greatest source of possible revenue in the colony was forbidden, just as it had been for many years.

The Powers That Be

The vast majority of the land in the colony was owned by the Penn family. Since 1660, when King Charles II had paid off a debt to William Penn by giving him the colony, Pennsylvania was known as a proprietary government, controlled not by the Crown, but by Penn and his descendants. The Penns were like absentee landlords, collecting rent on the millions of acres they owned. Penn's heirs lived in England; they appointed a royal governor to oversee their colony. The General Assembly had only as much power as the Penns chose to give it.

The thing that upset Franklin and the other members of the assembly was that the Penns paid no taxes on their property.

Those farmers who worked the land did pay, however, and they grew more dissatisfied with the arrangement as the Penn family in England became increasingly wealthy. As one historian writes, "The Penns believed that they were legally in the right. The Pennsylvanians were sure that they had reason and justice in their favor."[82]

William Penn, an Englishman, was given the colony of Pennsylvania by the king of England as payment for a debt. Penn and his family ruled the colony from England through an appointed colonial governor.

A brief Account of the

Province of **Pennsylvania,**

Lately Granted by the

KING,

Under the GREAT

Seal of England,

T O

WILLIAM PENN

AND HIS

Heirs and Assigns.

Since (by the good Providence of *God*, and the Favour of the *King*) a Country in *America* is fallen to my Lot, I thought it not less my Duty, then my Honest Interest, to give some publick notice of it to the World, that those of our own or other Nations, that are inclin'd to Transport Themselves or Families beyond the Seas, may find another Country added to their Choice; that if they shall happen to like the Place, Conditions, and Government, (so far as the present Infancy of things will allow us any prospect) they may, if they please, fix with me in the Province, hereafter described.

I. *The* KING'S *Title to this Country before he granted it.*

It is the *Jus Gentium*, or Law of Nations, that what ever Waste, or unculted Country, is the Discovery of any Prince, it is the right of that Prince that was at the Charge of the Discovery: Now this *Province* is a Member of that part of *America*, which the King of *Englands* Ancestors have been at the Charge of Discovering, and which they and he have taken great care to preserve and Improve.

A   II. William

The title page of William Penn's published account of how the American colony of Pennsylvania came to be under his dominion. The colonists thought that the Penns should pay taxes on their lands. The Penns disagreed.

The assembly tried several times to levy taxes on the Penns' land. However, the royal governor, acting as the Penns' representative, blocked every attempt. But as the war costs mounted, it became more clear to the assembly that, without taxing the Penns' land, there would not be enough money for adequate defense.

In an effort to bypass the governor, the General Assembly decided in 1757 to send an agent to England to talk to the Penns about changing the rules. Because of his ability to negotiate, Franklin was chosen as his colony's representative.

He was excited about going to England. He hoped that Deborah would make the journey with him, but she refused. She had a phobia about boats and sailing and knew she could never make the voyage. Franklin decided to take his twenty-seven-year-old son William along and leave Deborah and his thirteen-year-old daughter Sally at home. Franklin hoped to return to America in a few months.

A Failed Mission

Franklin's meeting with the Penns did not go well. He was known to Thomas and Richard Penn by reputation. They knew how he had worked with the Pennsylvania assembly for tax reform, and that angered them. The Penns also resented Franklin's popularity and his reputation as a genius.

He was so threatening to the Penns, in fact, that before Franklin even arrived from his twenty-seven-day voyage, Thomas Penn wrote to a friend in America, "Mr. Franklin's popularity is nothing here. . . . He will be looked very coldly upon by great people. . . . There are few of any consequence that have heard of his electrical experiments, those matters being attended to by a particular set of people."[83]

When the Philadelphian arrived in London he was met with rudeness and hostility. The Penns met with him several times but told Franklin that they refused to negotiate with him on the tax issue. They asked him to set out the assembly's petition in writing and said that their lawyers would consider it.

The petition was drawn up, but it lay unanswered for more than a year, while Franklin waited impatiently. Each time he inquired about its status, he was met with

MAKING ENEMIES ■ **75**

British aristocrat Richard Penn, son of William Penn, inherited, along with his brother Thomas, ownership of Pennsylvania. The Penn brothers saw Ben Franklin as a threat to their American financial interests.

vague answers, or none at all. Behind his back the Penns did what they could to tarnish his reputation in London. The Penns even wrote to the Pennsylvania General Assembly advising them to send a more qualified agent to London.

After more than two years of haggling, the Penns' lawyers worked out what they thought was a compromise, although it was a sorry one. A portion of the Penn land could be taxed, it was decided, but only at the lowest possible rate. Even so, hundreds of thousands of acres would remain tax free.

"Sensible, Virtuous, and Elegant Minds"

Even though the Penns' compromise officially completed Franklin's business in England, he remained there for two more years. He missed his family, he said, but he really loved Great Britain, and it was hard to leave.

The year Franklin had arrived in London, 1757, it was a busy, noisy city of 750,000 people. It was overcrowded and sooty, the skies were a perpetual grey from the pollution of coal fires, and it was crime ridden. Even so, it was one of the most vibrant cities in the world.

There were cafés and pubs and all kinds of places to meet friends. London was a hub of scientific thought. The theater, the symphony, and art galleries were exciting to the man from Philadelphia. In a letter to an English friend, Franklin said, "Why . . . should that little island [Great Britain] enjoy in almost every neighborhood, more sensible, virtuous, and elegant minds, than we can collect in ranging one hundred leagues of our vast forests?"[84]

Franklin enjoyed his life in London. He and William had found lodgings on Craven Street, in the home of a widow named Mary Stevenson. She and her daughter Polly became like a second family to Franklin; indeed, she seems to have taken over Deborah's role completely.

One historian writes, "She nursed Benjamin through a long illness, shopped for him uncomplainingly, commanded his servants and hers with a skill and efficiency always somehow beyond Deborah."[85] As to whether she and Franklin had a sexual relationship, historians don't agree.

Enjoying England

Franklin did keep up a regular correspondence with Deborah and Sally. And he sent gifts, too—lots of them. Yards of

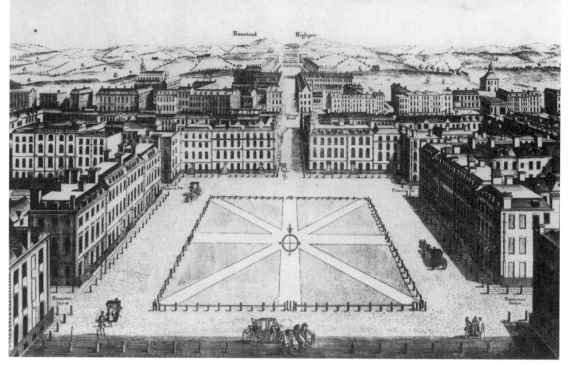

Hanover Square in eighteenth-century London. Franklin fell in love with London's sophistication and culture. He found it difficult to leave and return to more rustic Philadelphia.

expensive fabric for curtains and gowns, and books, musical instruments, and perfume were sent home to Philadelphia.

He even sent a big beer jug for which he had a special fondness. "I fell in love with it at first sight," he wrote to Deborah, "for I thought it looked like a fat jolly dame, clean and tidy, with a neat blue and white calico gown on, good-natured and lovely, and put me in mind of—somebody."[86]

Before leaving England Franklin and his son traveled around the countryside, looking up relatives from both his and Deborah's families. They traveled to Scotland, where he received an honorary doctorate degree from the University of St. Andrew's.

Franklin enrolled William in law school. He hoped that the boy would make a good lawyer. However, during the London years, William made a mistake: he fathered an illegitimate son. Historians have no idea who the mother was, but she gave William the infant, named William Temple Franklin, to raise.

Home to Philadelphia

When at last Franklin left England he had difficulty saying goodbye. He had made many friends and had cemented bonds with old friends. He told one of them that he planned to be back in England before two years' time elapsed.

There was plenty of work waiting for Franklin in Philadelphia. He was glad to see family and friends and eager to resume his old duties as postmaster (he had kept the position even during his absence). He also became involved with a more pressing problem—violence on the frontier—this time not from native Americans, but from Pennsylvania colonists.

In Franklin's absence hostility between the natives and colonists had worsened. As a reaction to this a mob of Scotch-Irish men calling themselves the Paxton Boys went on a killing spree. They moved into Lancaster County in 1764 and attacked a peaceful settlement of Conestoga (Susquehanna) people. Fourteen natives were killed, seven of them women and small children.

The incident resulted in outrage, from both the native Americans in the area and the English settlers. Franklin went to press with a pamphlet entitled "A Narrative of the Late Massacres in Lancaster County," which attacked the Paxton Boys and those who sympathized with them.

"What had little boys and girls done," Franklin demanded, "what could children a year old, babes at the breast, what could they do, that they too must be shot and hatcheted?—Horrid to relate—and in their parents' arms! This is done by no civilized nation in Europe. Do we come to America to learn and practice the manners of barbarians?"[87]

Even with public opinion against them the Paxton Boys continued their violence. They stormed toward the city of Philadelphia, vowing to shoot or hatchet to pieces the natives who were being protected there. Frightened out of his wits, the royal governor asked Franklin to ride out to meet the mob. Meanwhile, the citizens of the city prepared for battle.

Franklin did as the governor asked, taking a few men with him. He met the Paxton Boys at Germantown, eight miles from Philadelphia. Using his most stern, yet reasonable, tone, he explained to the

---

Air Baths

Franklin had very definite views about maintaining his health. In France, the fashion was cold baths, but he felt the cold water shocked his system, as this excerpt from Ronald Clark's biography of Franklin reveals.

"I have found it more agreeable to my constitution to bathe in another element, I mean cold air. . . . With this view I rise almost every morning, and sit in my chamber without any clothes whatever, half an hour or an hour, according to the season, either reading or writing. This practice is not in the least painful, but, on the contrary, agreeable; and if I return to bed afterwards, before I dress myself, as sometimes happens, I make a supplement to my night's rest of one or two hours of the most pleasing sleep that can be imagined."

---

mob that the city had assembled a huge defense against them and that an attack on Philadelphia would mean needless bloodshed.

Although unaccustomed to such danger Franklin did well in his confrontation. The Paxton Boys listened to what he said and turned back. In a letter to a friend in England, Franklin wrote about his adventure. "And within twenty-four hours," he said, "your old friend was a common soldier, a councillor, a kind of dictator, and ambassador to a country mob, and, on his returning home, nobody again."[88]

Disappointment and Hurt

Even with the many tasks Franklin had performed for the colony, he found himself in a close race in the assembly elections of 1764. Although many Pennsylvanians respected and admired him, he also had some enemies. The Scotch-Irish disliked him, and the Quakers were suspicious of him for his constant work to fortify the military. An especially vocal group of enemies was the Tories, a political party that was loyal to the Penns' proprietary government.

Franklin's political foes attempted to rally support among these groups to win the election. Opponents attacked his family, too, criticizing Franklin's humble beginnings and William's illegitimacy. The campaign was ugly, and in the end Franklin lost—by only twenty-five votes.

He was hurt and disappointed by the election. Nonetheless, he agreed to return to London when the assembly asked him to go as their agent once more. This time

he was to meet with the British government, not the Penns. His job was to request an end to the proprietary government; Pennsylvanians wished to become a Crown colony.

Once again he asked Deborah to accompany him, but once more she declined. Historians say that it might have been for the best. She was barely literate and would have had difficulty moving in the same intellectual circles as her husband. Because she looked up to him, she called Franklin "her old Pappy," and he constantly referred to her as "my dear child."[89]

As before his last voyage to England, he assured Deborah that his business would take no more than six months to complete. This time, too, he was incorrect in his estimate. He would be gone more than ten years; Deborah would be dead when he returned.

The Stamp Act

Socially, Franklin picked up where he left off in England. He moved back into Mary Stevenson's lodgings and saw old friends. However, the petition he carried to the British government had to be set aside, for there were more pressing problems for Franklin and the American colonies.

While Franklin had been making his voyage to England in December 1764, Parliament was hard at work, exploring ways to raise money, for England was short of funds. The long war in America against the French and Indians had cost the country dearly. It was important to make up the lost money, but the question was, How? As

Franklin's boat docked in England, the British had found their answer—the American colonies.

They proposed a new tax, called the Stamp Act. It required that a special seal, or stamp, be affixed to all official documents, diplomas, and licenses—even playing cards. This stamp added an extra cost to the item, ranging from a few pennies to several pounds. In all, fifty-five items commonly purchased in the colonies would require such stamps.

Franklin did not like the idea of adding another burden to the colonists, who were already paying heavy taxes to their colonial governments. He arranged a meeting with the British minister of finance, George Grenville, to try to talk Grenville out of pursuing the tax. But Franklin could not persuade him, and the Stamp Act became law in 1765.

In 1765, England's Parliament decreed that all colonial documents must be stamped with a seal like this and that a tax be paid to get the seal. The colonists reacted violently to the new tax—a reaction that would eventually lead to revolution.

Surprising Reactions

Franklin was usually known for his shrewd ability to gauge people's emotions. However, he greatly underestimated the colonists' reaction to the Stamp Act, and he paid for his mistake.

Franklin urged the colonies to take the situation calmly and with a sense of compromise. The Stamp Act was just another tax. There was nothing new about taxing documents and licenses. In England people had had such a tax for years.

To John Hughes, a friend in Philadelphia, who had written Franklin about the colonies' anger, he wrote, "A firm loyalty to the Crown and faithful adherence to the government of this nation, which it is the safety as well as honor of the colonies to be connected with, will always be the wiser course for you and I to take."[90]

But the colonists were furious that Parliament should dare to tax them. It was not just the idea of a new tax, it was the *way* in which they were being taxed. Parliament was a legislative body in which the colonies had absolutely no representation. If Parliament could levy taxes and enact unpleasant laws with no one to object, the colonies were completely powerless. It was bad enough to pay taxes to their colonial governments, but at least there they were able to send elected representatives.

In Boston, Philadelphia, and other colonial cities there were riots and angry demonstrations. Because Franklin had not denounced the Stamp Act loudly enough and was urging compromise and moderation, anger was aimed at him, too. He was called a traitor and a collaborator with the British government.

An English lithograph of 1774 depicts one fate that often awaited the royal tax collector in the American colonies. Vengeful colonists tarred and feathered this one, then poured the heavily taxed tea down his throat.

In Philadelphia an angry mob threatened to storm his house on Market Street. Deborah, hearing of the danger, sent Sally to safety at a friend's house. But Deborah, along with two male relatives, armed themselves with guns and knives and waited for the mob, which was finally turned away.

The news of such reactions finally reached Franklin in London. He wrote to Deborah, telling her how proud he was that she was brave enough to stand up to the angry townspeople. "I honor much the spirit and courage you showed, and the prudent preparations you made in that time of danger," he said. "The woman deserves a good house that is determined to defend it."[91]

From Goat to Hero

Now that Franklin understood the mood of the colonies in America toward the Stamp Act, he began a determined effort

---

Celebrating the Repeal

Franklin celebrated the repeal of the Stamp Act by buying gifts for his family, which he described in a letter to Deborah in April 1766, and which Esmond Wright quotes in his biography.

"As the Stamp Act is at length repealed, I am willing you should have a new gown, which you may suppose I did not send sooner, as I knew you would not like to be finer than your neighbors, unless in a gown of your own spinning. . . . I have sent you a fine piece of pompador satin, 14 yards, cost 11 shillings per yard; a silk negligee and petticoat of brocaded lustring [surface] for my dear Sally, with two dozen gloves, 4 bottles of lavender water, and two little reels [of silk thread]."

to get it repealed. Fortunately, there were plenty of businessmen in England who were unsure about the wisdom of such a tax. They worried that if the colonists became angry enough, it might result in a boycott of their products. Since the colonics provided the bulk of their business, they knew a boycott would be disastrous.

As a result of the controversy a meeting was called in Britain's House of Commons to discuss the Stamp Act. The government heard witnesses testify about the law and the effects it could have. Franklin was to be the key witness. Historians say that it was one of his most masterful appearances.

His testimony began with a clerk's question, "What is your name and place of abode?" Franklin, in a solemn, strong voice answered, "Franklin of Philadelphia." So began a grueling, four-hour examination by George Grenville, the British minister of finance.

Franklin had prepared carefully for this meeting. He had gathered facts and figures and committed them to memory so that he would not be bound to notes. Shrewdly he had also planted questions among his friends in the House of Commons. The answers to these questions were important, and he was not willing to risk Grenville's failure to ask them.

He told the chamber how the Stamp Act would do nothing but cause hostility and resentment among the colonists, who had always had the utmost respect and loyalty to the Crown. He also reminded them that the colonists were more than willing to boycott British goods if they were pushed hard enough.

One exchange between a member of the House of Commons and Franklin pointed this out:

Angry colonial taxpayers soon went beyond tarring and feathering royal tax collectors. In this engraving from 1774, a lynch mob kidnaps the local tax collector and hangs him.

Laying It on the Line

Members of the House of Commons listened carefully to the answers Franklin gave to certain questions during the Stamp Act controversy. One of the most interesting was the question posed by Franklin's friend Grey Cooper—planted by Franklin ahead of time, and quoted by Catherine Bowen in her book, The Most Dangerous Man in America.

"Q: What was the temper of Americans toward Great Britain before the year 1763?

A: The best in the world. They submitted willingly to the government of the crown, and paid, in all their courts, obedience to acts of parliament. . . . They were led by a thread. They had not only a respect, but an affection, for Great Britain, for its laws, its customs and manners, and even a fondness for its fashions, that greatly increased the commerce. Natives of Great Britain were always treated with particular regard; to be an Old Englandman was, of itself, a character of some respect, and gave a kind of rank among us.

Q: And what is their temper now?

A: Oh, very much altered."

Question: What used to be the pride of the Americans?

Franklin: To indulge in the fashions and manufactures of Great Britain.

Question: What is now their pride?

Franklin: To wear their old clothes over again, till they can make new ones.[92]

Due to Franklin's testimony and reactions across the Atlantic in America, the Stamp Act was repealed in February 1766. Throughout the colonies people cheered Franklin, drinking toasts to his genius and brave spirit. Never had jeers turned so quickly to praise.

But Franklin's reaction was bittersweet. He was glad that for the moment the British had had the good sense to back away from a potentially ruinous mistake. But all was not well. The tax, he knew, was not the issue. The British government still maintained that it had the right—whenever it chose to do so—to tax the colonies.

An enormous amount of energy had been spent in fighting off the Stamp Act. But what would be the next fight? And at what price?

8 Moving Toward War

Following his appearance in the House of Commons, Franklin sent off a message to the Pennsylvania General Assembly, saying that he wanted to return home. But the assembly asked him to stay on as their agent.

Colonial leader Patrick Henry uttered the immortal "Give me liberty or give me death." Such sentiments among the colonies made Franklin's diplomatic tasks more difficult.

There were new controversies between the colonies and the British government that were troublesome, and the assembly believed that Franklin's presence in London might be helpful.

The colonies were upset over another British edict known as the Quartering Act. This act required the colonists to house and pay for the expenses of a standing army of British troops stationed in America. The New York assembly refused, and other colonies threatened to follow suit, since the law had come from Parliament without the consent of the colonies.

Because of his presence and status in England, Franklin was rapidly becoming a spokesman for all of the American colonies. In fact, three other colonies besides Pennsylvania asked him to be their official agent in London—New Jersey, Massachusetts, and Georgia.

"So Many Inattentive Heads"

Deborah Franklin, meanwhile, waited hopefully for her husband to return. Each year that passed, she grew more disappointed. "I am in the dark," she wrote sadly to Franklin in 1767, "and my life of old age is one continued state of suspense."[93]

Anger at England

After being verbally abused by Britain's Alexander Wedderburn in front of the Privy Council, Franklin wrote to his friend Thomas Cushing on February 15, 1774, that he was more angry about how the situation affected the colonists than for his own reputation.

"It may be supposed that I am very angry on this occasion. . . . But indeed, what I feel on my own account is half lost in what I feel for the public. When I see that all petitions and complaints of grievances are so odious to the government that even the mere pipe which conveys them becomes obnoxious, I am at a loss to know how peace and union are to be maintained or restored between the different parts of the empire.

Grievances cannot be redressed unless they are known; and they cannot be known but through complaints and petitions. If these are deemed affronts, and the messengers punished as offenders, who will henceforth send petitions? And who will deliver them?"

At the same time, Franklin was combining diplomatic business with travel in Europe. He visited France and thoroughly enjoyed it. He met the king, and he was introduced to many of the leading French scientists of the day. The French respected Franklin more than did the English.

As the months passed and no progress was made in resolving problems between England and the colonies, Franklin felt less useful. He wrote to his son in New Jersey, "I am weary of suggesting [ideas] to so many inattentive heads, though I must do it while I am among them."[94]

His voice was one of compromise. But it was an increasingly difficult position to maintain. The British government was losing patience with the headstrong colonies and wanted to hear nothing from Franklin about the rights of Americans. And across the Atlantic important colonial leaders such as Patrick Henry and Samuel Adams were calling for a split from Great Britain. Compromise was not on their minds, either.

A Fair Hit

In an attempt to garner support and poke fun at these new British edicts, Franklin used a tactic that had served him well in the past—humor.

Using the name King Frederick, Franklin wrote an open letter to the British people, which was published in a London newspaper. Entitled "Edict of King Frederick of Prussia," the letter reminded the British that their land had been colonized by Prussians. Therefore, wrote King Frederick, Prussia has a right to make laws for

Great Britain and to tax British people. The king went on to give orders he expected the British to follow, such as sending all their iron ore and fur pelts to Prussia to be processed. Sarcastically, he assured the British that they would be welcome to buy the finished products, at full price.

All of these remarks, of course, were based on the orders that Great Britain was giving the American colonies. Not all the British saw it as a joke. When the letter was published Franklin was having breakfast with some friends in London. He later wrote to his son William that one of the men believed the letter to be true and worried that King Frederick might soon be on the march toward England.

Franklin wrote that another friend, Paul Whitehead, "who is very shrewd . . . soon after began to [figure out the hoax],

From England Franklin corresponded with Samuel Adams during unrest in Boston.

and looking in my face said, 'I'll be hanged if this is not some of your American jokes on us.'" As the friends continued reading the letter, the group "ended with an abundance of laughing, and a general verdict that it was a fair hit."[95]

"I Have Been Saucy"

While some of Franklin's English friends enjoyed the hoax, many in the British government were annoyed with the Philadelphian, thinking him disloyal. They began to call him Judas on Craven Street. Franklin wrote to his sister Jane in Boston that he was becoming bored with his role as diplomat, always having to be congenial to people he had no use for:

> I had used all the smooth words I could muster, and I grew tired of meekness when I saw it without effect. Of late, therefore, I have been saucy, and in two papers . . . I have held up a looking glass in which some ministers [government officials] may see their ugly faces. . . . And there is truth in the old saying that if you make yourself a sheep, the wolves will eat you.[96]

His sauciness came out occasionally in the letters he sent to America. Not *in* the letters, really, but *on* the letters. As postmaster he was allowed free postage on any letter he sent. He normally wrote "Free" before his name, "B. Franklin," in the upper right-hand corner of the envelope. As he became more irritated with the British government, however, he began rearranging the words to "B. Free Franklin," both to annoy the British and to keep up morale in the colonies.

It was harder for Franklin to be an effective diplomat, for events in the colonies did not lend themselves to be settled by compromise. British oppression of the colonies was getting heavier. In March 1770 five colonists were killed by British soldiers during an angry mob scene in Boston. Although historians say the soldiers shot out of fear for their lives, the incident soon became known as the Boston Massacre. The people of Massachusetts were furious, and they raged against the British government.

The British, on the other hand, had only Franklin to rail against. What were those colonists doing? How dare they defy orders of the British government! Although frustrated himself, Franklin tried to keep the fragile relationship between himself and the British government from shattering.

But it did shatter, due to a series of letters known as the Hutchinson letters. So important were they, in fact, that the prime minister of England, Lord North, would state, "These [letters] brought on the war."[97]

The Hutchinson Letters and a Tea Party

Thomas Hutchinson was the royal governor of Massachusetts, an American appointed by the Crown. While in England Franklin somehow got possession of some letters that Hutchinson had written to a British official. In the letters Hutchinson said that the colonists had too much freedom and

Bostonians posted this angry response to the Boston Massacre and other events in 1770.

Sir Frederick North, prime minister of England in 1773, cited the publication of the so-called Hutchinson letters as a chief reason for the American Revolution.

called for "an abridgement of what is called English liberty."[98]

Franklin was furious that an American would be collaborating with the British to place stricter limits on the colonies. He decided to send the letters to colonial activist Samuel Adams and certain others in America—not to be published, but to be studied and thought about. One thing the letters might do, Franklin thought, was to reassure the colonial leaders that it was not always the English who were the villains.

Franklin also intended to present a public petition to the British government from the people of Massachusetts for the removal of Hutchinson. The British ministers had no intention of recalling the royal governor, but they agreed to let Franklin plead his case. But before the matter could go any further, the colonists took their frustrations about the British government into their own hands by staging a rebellious "tea party" in Boston Harbor in 1773.

Angered by more British restrictions, rebellious colonists calling themselves The Sons of Liberty stormed onto British cargo ships in the middle of the night. The ships held crates of tea, which Britain

During the Boston Tea Party of 1773, Bostonians, angry over new taxes, raided ships laden with tea and dumped the tea into the harbor. In England, Franklin denounced this action and sought to make amends for it.

John Adams, a colonial leader in Massachusetts and, later, the second president of the United States, denounced the royal governor, Thomas Hutchinson, as a "vile serpent."

the [Hutchinson] letters, they were doomed to be public property."[100] The letters, along with a scathing attack on Hutchinson, were published in the *Boston Gazette* for all the colonists to see.

The reaction was similar to setting a spark to a powder keg. People throughout America fumed that they had been betrayed by one of their own. One of the colonial leaders, John Adams, wrote in his diary about Hutchinson, "Cool, thinking, deliberate villain. Born of our bone, born and educated among us . . . vile serpent."[101]

The government was angry at Franklin because of publication of the Hutchinson letters. The British resolved to censure Franklin publicly for his distribution of the letters.

ordered the colonies to pay taxes on. Rather than go along with what they felt was an unfair new law, the colonists dumped tons of the tea into the waters of Boston Harbor.

Interestingly, Franklin was outspoken against the Boston Tea Party. He called it "an act of violent injustice"[99] and worried that such violence would ruin chances for a peaceful settlement. He urged the Massachusetts assembly to reimburse Britain for the ruined tea. He even told British ministers that he would pay for the tea himself—on one condition: he demanded that Parliament repeal some of its strictest new laws against the colonists. No one in British government was in the mood to bargain.

Meanwhile, something else happened that could never have been foreseen by Franklin. As Catherine Drinker Bowen writes, "As soon as Sam Adams laid eyes on

The Scapegoat

The scene for this censure was a meeting before Britain's Privy Council, an elite body of the king's most trusted counselors, to be held in January 1774. It was clear within a few moments that the purpose of the meeting was to humiliate and verbally abuse Franklin.

The main speaker for the government was a hawk-nosed Scottish lawyer named Alexander Wedderburn. With the lords and ministers and their supporters looking on in amusement, Wedderburn pounded his fists on the table and shouted at Franklin. "I hope, my lords, you will mark and brand this man for the honor of this country, of Europe, and of mankind. . . . He has forfeited all the respect of societies and men."[102]

Franklin (left center) stands before the king's Privy Council in January 1774. He was publicly censured and humiliated by the council, which blamed him for the publication of the Hutchinson letters. The letters' publication ignited violence in the colonies.

For an hour Wedderburn screamed dozens of insults at Franklin, calling him a thief and a liar, as the rest of the Privy Council jeered and laughed. Franklin, dressed in a brown velvet coat, stood quietly before the council, not saying a word.

Later, in a letter to his son William back in New Jersey, Franklin said that he "made no return of the injury by abusing my adversaries, but held a cool, sullen silence."[103] And though Wedderburn's remarks were printed and circulated in England and the colonies in an attempt to further damage his reputation, Franklin said that the most vicious parts of Wedderburn's tirade were left out. "The grosser parts of the abuse are omitted, appearing, I suppose, in their own eyes, too foul to be seen on paper."[104]

Going Home

There was no question after this incident that Franklin's business in England was finished. The British government stripped him of his position as deputy postmaster of the colonies. There was even talk of putting him in jail; indeed, Franklin told a friend that he considered burning all his personal papers.

As he was preparing for his voyage home early in 1775, he received more bad news. Deborah had died several weeks before. Six months earlier he had written to Deborah, assuring her that he hoped to be on his way home by summer, and to find her "well and hearty . . . when I have the happiness once more of seeing you."[105]

With his dream of reconciling British and American differences in shambles, and with the loss of his wife, Franklin must have felt miserable. On his last day in England he sat with a friend, Joseph Priestly. Franklin was reading newspapers from the colonies. Priestly noted later that "Now and then the philosopher could not read for the tears that filled his eyes and ran down his cheeks."[106]

The Continental Congressman

Franklin arrived home in Philadelphia on May 5, 1775; the very next day he was unanimously chosen to represent Pennsylvania in the Second Continental Congress. The Continental Congress was a body of legislators that had recently been formed from individual colonial assemblies. The Continental Congress met to evaluate the growing crisis with England and to find ways to keep the colonies united in their protests against the Crown. The work of the congress had increased as relations with Britain had deteriorated.

Franklin was sixty-nine years old—quite elderly by standards of the day. Nevertheless, he was given a great deal of work to do. In addition to his congressional post he was appointed postmaster general of the colonies, a post the British crown had recently taken from him. He was also chosen as one of three commissioners whose job was to gain Canada's support for a colonial revolution.

Franklin designed a paper currency for use in all the colonies and worked with John Adams and Thomas Jefferson in creating the Great Seal, to be used on all official American documents. (That seal, a rather mysterious picture of an eye over a pyramid, is used today on the back of U.S. one-dollar bills.)

He also sat down with Gen. George Washington to form the new Continental army, making decisions about uniforms, salary, organization of ranks, and even the use of certain weapons. He seriously suggested the use of bows and arrows by the American soldiers, since they were quieter and more dependable than guns at the time.

And while many in the Continental Congress relished Franklin's wisdom and admired his humor and energy, others were peeved at his popularity. John Adams

Gen. George Washington reviews the troops of the newly formed Continental army. Benjamin Franklin worked with Washington on the formation and organization of the army.

complained in his diary that Franklin's role in the Revolution would almost certainly be exaggerated, telling the story that "Franklin's electrical rod smote the earth and out sprang George Washington. . . . Franklin electrified him with his rod—and thenceforth these two conducted all the policy negotiations, legislatures and war."[107]

Heartache

If Franklin cared about such petty jealousies he spent little time worrying about them. More personal matters occupied his mind. Franklin was finding that he and his son were on opposite sides of the coming Revolution.

William Franklin had very different views from his father. Months before Franklin had written to William in New Jersey, urging him to resign as royal governor there. It would, said Franklin, be a good show of unity for the colonial cause.

William refused, urging his father to resign from the Continental Congress, instead. He told his father that he considered himself a loyal British subject and held in "the utmost contempt" those who would betray Great Britain.[108]

As the colonies moved closer to declaring their independence, William was placed under house arrest, considered an enemy of the people. This was a source of shame and embarrassment to his father, who, as one historian wrote, "carried his hurt to the grave."[109]

A Painful Split

The political differences between Franklin and his son William were enormous. Franklin found it difficult to forgive William for his staunch loyalty to the British government. After the war, when William had moved to England, he wrote to his father in July 1784, asking if they could meet. Franklin's reply was cool.

"Indeed nothing has ever hurt me so much and affected me with such keen sensations, as to find myself deserted in my old age by my only son; and not only deserted, but to find him taking up arms against me, in a cause wherein my good fame, fortune, and life were all at stake. You conceived, you say, that your duty to your king and regard for your country required this. I ought not to blame you for differing in sentiment with me in public affairs. We are men, all subject to errors. . . . Your situation was such that few would have censured your remaining neuter, though there are natural duties which precede political ones, and cannot be extinguished by them. This is a disagreeable subject. I drop it. . . . I shall be glad to see you when convenient, but would not have you come here at present."

Editing and Signing

In 1776 the Continental Congress finally voted to formally declare the colonies independent from England. Thomas Jefferson was chosen to write the declaration, and Franklin was asked to edit it. Jefferson mentioned in his diary that the only reason Franklin was not asked to write the document was that nobody could trust him not to put a joke in it.

Jefferson was himself a brilliant writer, but he did have difficulty accepting Franklin's professional criticism. Franklin actually made few changes in the original manuscript, but one in particular bothered Jefferson. The original stated, "We hold these truths to be sacred and undeniable." Always eager to pare unnecessary words whenever possible, Franklin crossed out "sacred and undeniable" and added "self-evident."

There was some Franklin humor at the formal signing of the Declaration of Independence on August 2, 1776, and it had to do with the danger the men faced as visible leaders of the Revolution. According to John Hancock of Massachusetts, at the conclusion of the signing Franklin said, "Gentlemen, we must now hang together, or we shall most assuredly hang separately!"[110]

It was, as Hancock pointed out, a joke. But there was more than a little truth to the fact that America was on a very dangerous road. With Great Britain—the most powerful nation in the world—as adversary, the colonies had passed the point of no return.

9 The Diplomat in Paris

Declaring independence from Britain in writing was only the beginning for the American colonies. Great Britain had no intention of giving up its colonies without a fight. And late in 1776 the Americans seemed to be losing that fight. British troops had occupied New York; Washington's Continental army was in retreat.

"I am Old and Good for Nothing"

It was clear to the members of the Continental Congress that they could not win the war without outside help. The congress decided in September to send three commissioners to Paris to seek a treaty of alliance with the French king. Franklin was their first choice; they also asked Silas Deane and Arthur Lee, both of whom were already in Europe.

Franklin was seventy years old, and the thought of another ocean voyage was not pleasant. "I am old and good for nothing,"[111] he leaned over and said to Benjamin Rush at the meeting of the congress. However, he vowed he would do what he could to help secure assistance from the French.

On October 26, 1776, Franklin sailed to France aboard the *Reprisal,* an Ameri-

can ship. With him were his two grandsons—William Temple Franklin, now sixteen, and Benjamin Franklin Bache, daughter Sally's seven-year-old son. Temple, as the older boy was called, was going along as his grandfather's personal secretary. Little Benny was going to attend school in Geneva, Switzerland.

The journey was potentially dangerous, for there were British ships skulking off the American coast, waiting to attack colonial ships. To capture one of the Crown's worst enemies at sea would have been an honor for a British sea captain.

Even with the possibility of capture Franklin enjoyed the trip. As he had with other transatlantic trips, he spent much of his time in scientific pursuits. As Van Doren writes, "The indomitable old man, who was almost certain to be hanged for high treason if the *Reprisal* should be captured, noted the temperature of air and water every day, again studying the Gulf Stream."[112]

The *Reprisal* docked in France on December 3. Sick and weak from the sea voyage, Franklin had difficulty standing up when he got off the ship. But his journey was far from over. From the seaport it was a long 320 miles to Paris. At towns along the way the American was greeted by cheering crowds, who hoped to get a look at this famous man who had accomplished so much in his lifetime. After seventeen days an exhausted Franklin arrived at the French capital.

A Tough Mission

The French government had been helping the colonists all along, but secretly. They had set up a phony import firm called Hortalez and Company that shipped weapons to the Caribbean, where American ships would pick them up. Over $400,000's worth of war materials had been sent to the colonists this way.

But no more aid was forthcoming. The French government sympathized with the colonies, but they did not want to throw money away on a losing proposition. The French king, Louis XVI, hated the successor to George II, English George III, but he was uneasy in the role of openly supporting rebellion against any monarch.

The French foreign minister, Comte de Vergennes, shared his king's hatred of the British. He wanted revenge for the

An elderly Ben Franklin, supported on either side by his grandsons, makes his way through the streets of Paris as crowds cheer him.

A lady of the French court teases Franklin for not wearing a powdered white wig, as fashion dictated.

pounding that French forces took at the hands of the English in the French and Indian War. Vergennes knew, too, that if the Americans were successful in their revolution, it would cripple Great Britain.

France had other concerns before it would agree to a formal alliance. The government needed assurance that the colonies had a good chance of winning their war. For if they lost, a victorious England would doubtlessly turn on any European allies of the colonies.

Franklin met regularly with Vergennes, reminding him of how valuable a trading partner America would be once the colonies were free of British restrictions. He also warned the foreign minister how all-powerful the British government would be if they were to win the war.

"Among the Powdered Heads of France"

Diplomacy was a slow business, and Franklin wisely understood that it would do no good to rush the French minister.

He could only wait for news from the colonies, hoping that Washington and his army could somehow gain the upper hand and give Vergennes and Louis XVI the assurances they needed.

While he waited he enjoyed Paris and the surrounding countryside. He stayed in a wing of a beautiful estate in Passy, a village two miles outside Paris. He was fascinated with the landscape, the different plants and animals, and most of all, the people. And much to his surprise the people loved him.

When he had first arrived he had been ill and had taken no care with his appearance as he traveled. He was dressed in old, frumpy clothes, a worn fur hat, and no wig—although wigs were standard fashion of the day.

In a letter to a friend, Franklin wrote, "Figure me in your mind as jolly as formerly, and as strong and hearty, only a few years older; very plainly dressed, wearing my thin, gray, straight hair that peeps out under . . . a fine fur cap, which comes down my forehead almost to my spectacles. Think how this must appear among the powdered heads of Paris!"[113]

But the people adored him. They gathered outside his room, hoping to touch his coat or to get a word from him. Franklin was shrewd enough to use his popularity to his advantage. He continued to wear the same old clothes, and he never put on a wig. His fur hat became sort of a symbol—the old, eccentric American. Because of his simplicity he seemed all the more lovable.

Throughout France, in every shop, pictures of Franklin in his hat and brown coat adorned the shelves. On snuff boxes, plates, statues—everywhere was the image of Benjamin Franklin. He was asked to sit for portraits "so often I am perfectly sick of it," he wrote to a friend.[114]

Not all of his encounters in France were pleasant, however. At a country inn Franklin ran into historian Edward Gibbon, who wrote the famous *The History of the Decline and Fall of the Roman Empire*. On noticing that Gibbon was waiting to be served in the inn, Franklin sent a servant to invite Gibbon to dine with him.

Gibbon was British, and a member of Parliament. He sent word back to Franklin that he could never have polite conversation with a rebel against the king of England. Franklin, so the story goes, sent back regrets, and added that if Mr. Gibbon every decided to write a book on the decline and fall of the British Empire, Franklin would be happy to supply him "with ample materials."[115]

Good News

The British government, with its network of spies, knew all about Franklin's activities in France. They were well aware of his petitions for aid, and the British ministers in London were furious. They reminded Comte de Vergennes that by helping the Americans, France would be declaring war on England. Vergennes understood. However, he continued to walk a tightrope with

---

Simplicity and Innocence

Franklin's appearance while in Paris was described by the French historian Hilliard d'Auberteuil, as quoted by Esmond Wright in Franklin *of Philadelphia.*

"Everything in him announced the simplicity and the innocence of primitive morals. . . . He showed to the astonished multitude a head worthy of the brush of Guide [a painter of old men] on an erect and vigorous body, clad in the simplest of garments. His eyes were shadowed by large glasses and in his hand he carried a white cane. He spoke little. He knew how to be impolite without being rude, and his pride seemed to be that of nature. Such a person was made to excite the curiosity of Paris. The people clustered around as he passed and asked, 'Who is this old peasant who has such a noble air?'"

The Battle of Saratoga (above) ended in a major victory for the Continental army. British general Burgoyne surrendered (right) with six thousand troops.

Franklin, keeping the war aid as secret as he could.

Finally there was good news from America. On December 4, 1777, Franklin received word that the British general Burgoyne had been defeated soundly at Saratoga, in upstate New York. Six thousand British troops surrendered—a major victory for the Continental army.

Franklin rushed to Comte de Vergennes. Surely this was the turning point, the signal the French had been looking for that Americans could win the war. Unfortunately, the French minister had to delay signing any alliance. He would sign, he assured Franklin, but only if Spain would also sign.

Spain was a close ally of France. Too, the Spanish king was a relative of Louis XVI, and the alliance was a strong one. But Spain had objections to signing an alliance with the American colonies. There were Spanish colonies in Central and South America. Any whisper of revolution might set off the same thing in those Spanish colonies.

A Little Trickery

Franklin was worried. He knew that the alliance couldn't wait, that France had to be pushed a little harder. He resorted to a little trickery.

He knew that a British spy named Paul Wentworth was in Paris. Wentworth's mission was to try to find out whatever he could about Franklin's activities. Franklin ordinarily would have ignored the spy, but instead he invited him to dinner.

Franklin knew that the French would be nervous about such a meeting, wondering whether Britain and America were working out some sort of truce. If they were, would the two nations create an alliance that might be turned on France?

Franklin used this fear to his advantage. He and Wentworth had dinner and talked very generally about the war. (Franklin was also careful to leave a "confidential" letter on his table, knowing that Wentworth would read it as soon as Franklin left the room.)

When the dinner was over Franklin received word from Comte de Vergennes. It no longer mattered that the Spanish government was reluctant to agree to the alliance. The French, said Vergennes, were ready to sign.

A Little Revenge

It took several weeks for the details of the alliance to be worked out. Franklin, in an old brown velvet coat, arrived for the formal signing on February 5, 1778—only to be informed that the minister was sick in bed with a cold. The following day Franklin appeared again, wearing the same coat.

His colleague Silas Deane commented on the fact that he was wearing the same coat two consecutive days—strange even for Franklin. Franklin smiled and explained why it was important for him to wear that coat to such an important occasion. "To give it a little revenge," he told Deane. "I wore this coat on the day Wedderburn abused me at Whitehall."[116]

Hard Feelings

The alliance with France was a great moment for Franklin. But even with French assistance, he had worries about the success of the American colonies. The Continental Congress was not always smart about the ways it allocated funds. Often its use of money was downright wasteful. No matter how much money France agreed to provide to the war effort, misuse of it by the congress would not help the colonies at all.

It worried him, too, that the congress had a habit of spending French money before Franklin had actually received it. In a letter to a fellow congressman, Franklin complained that "the storm of bills [from America] has terrified and vexed me to such a degree that I am deprived of sleep."[117]

Too, there were times when egos got in the way of the Americans. Franklin was one of three American commissioners sent by the American colonies. Because of his age and reputation, Franklin was the most influential of the three, a fact that sometimes caused resentment with one of the other commissioners, a Virginian named Arthur Lee.

Lee was a jealous man, resentful of the fact that Franklin had gotten so much of the credit for the French alliance. To vent his anger Lee wrote letters to the Continental Congress accusing his fellow commissioners of accepting bribes from the French, saying that both Deane, the other commissioner, and "the old doctor [Franklin] . . . [were] concerned in the plunder, and . . . in time we shall collect the proofs."[118]

Franklin usually could ignore pettiness, but in a letter to Arthur Lee he unleashed his fury. Franklin said that he had "often received and borne your magisterial snubbings and rebukes" and that he had done so "out of pity for your sick mind, which is forever tormenting itself with its jealousies, suspicions, and fancies that others mean you ill." He also warned Lee, "If you do not cure yourself of this temper, it will end in insanity."[119]

Eventually, sensing the problem with the three commissioners, the Continental Congress decided that only one representative of the colonies was needed in Paris. Franklin became the sole American minister, much to Lee's displeasure.

The Job of a Diplomat

Franklin's major responsibility after the signing of the alliance was to keep the money flowing across the Atlantic. Millions of dollars in French cash and goods had reached the colonies by 1782. Historians are in agreement that the war could never have been won without such assistance.

But there were other tasks Franklin had to perform. Once the French got into the war a steady stream of Europeans wanted to go and fight for the colonial cause. They saw it as a noble effort against a common foe; many saw it as a chance to earn money in an exciting way. They came to France to apply for a commission in the Continental army. Franklin was the man they saw.

Often the applicants were good soldiers with records of bravery and courage. The sole qualification of many others, however, was knowing someone in the French government, and Franklin felt obligated to accept them, too. He wrote a letter to Washington, apologizing for having to make such "clearly political choices."[120]

Franklin had a good eye for character, though, and there were some valu-

Benjamin Franklin recruited revolutionary naval hero John Paul Jones in France. Jones named his ship the Bonhomme Richard, *in honor of Franklin's famous almanac.*

able additions to Washington's army that came from Franklin's recommendations. One was daredevil Scottish sea captain John Paul Jones, who named his warship *Bonhomme Richard* (French for "Good Man Richard") in honor of Franklin and his famous almanac. Jones fought and won key sea battles against the British. Another was French nobleman Marquis de Lafayette, a confident young officer who became one of Washington's most trusted soldiers.

Franklin also sent a forty-seven-year old German captain named Friedrich von Steuben to Washington. It was Steuben whose attention to detail and ceaseless drills turned Washington's ragtag army into a well-organized fighting machine.

Franklin recognized that German captain Friedrich von Steuben would be an asset to Washington's army. Steuben turned a collection of colonial rebels into a disciplined army.

Electrocuting England and Other Tricks

Although winning independence from England was all important to Franklin, he kept the war in perspective. He was quick to issue safe-conduct passes for British ships that had no connection to the fighting, such as those carrying food or supplies to other British colonies. He also warned French and American ships to stay clear of Capt. James Cook's ship. Cook was a famous geographer and explorer who had nothing whatsoever to do with the war.

Franklin's reputation as a scientist played a small part in the war, too. Rumors about special weapons he had supposedly invented circulated at various times throughout the war, and many were actually believed.

The report of two such inventions was relayed to England by a spy in France. According to the spy Franklin had built "a great number of reflecting mirrors which will reflect so much heat from the sun as they will destroy anything by fire at a very considerable distance." The report goes on to say that Franklin had the giant mirrors aimed at the British coast, where "they mean to burn and destroy the whole navy of Great Britain in our harbors."

In addition, wrote the nervous British agent, Franklin had a chain stretched from England to the French coast. During the panic that would ensue during the mirror fire, Franklin "with a prodigious electrical machine of his own invention, will convey such a shock as will entirely overturn our whole island."[121]

Of course such a report had no basis in fact, but it does indicate how highly Franklin's scientific genius was regarded.

Running from Court to Court

It seemed, by 1780, that the Continental Congress was like a deep pit into which Franklin threw French money. It was a never-ending task for him, and he hated it. "I have long been humiliated," he wrote to John Adams, "with the idea of our running about from court to court begging for money."[122]

He wrote often to the congress to be more thrifty and discriminating in how they spent the money. But a letter arrived from General Washington that deeply disturbed Franklin. Washington wrote that money was scarce, that his soldiers had not been paid in months. If the situation did not improve quickly, Washington warned, there would be mutiny.

Franklin knew the answer was to send the money to Washington directly, for the general would know just how it was to be spent. To avoid the middleman—the Continental Congress—he talked Louis XVI into parting with millions of dollars for the Continental army. It was not a loan, but a gift, and Franklin so stipulated in his letter to the congress.

Franklin knew that the congress would be annoyed that they were left out of the process—after all, spending and allocating funds was one of their most important jobs. But Franklin reminded them that the money was a gift, and that every gift giver had "the right of qualifying his gifts with such terms as he thinks proper."[123]

The War Ends

Finally happy news reached Franklin in Paris. British general Cornwallis had been caught between eighteen thousand French and American troops. Cornwallis and his men had been forced to surrender, marking the end of the war.

Franklin was relieved, although he understood that his job was not yet over. It was important that he remain in France while peace negotiations were worked out between the British government and the colonies. As it turned out those negotiations took another two years.

Franklin led the negotiating. From the outset he was tough and unyielding, and except for one point concerning the yielding of Canada to America, he was able to write almost every bit of the treaty to American specifications. When at last the Treaty of Paris was signed on September 3, 1783, America was finally free and independent. This pleased the French government, for it weakened their British rival.

Lord Cornwallis (right) was commander of the British forces during the American Revolution. Caught between French and American troops, he surrenders (above) on October 19, 1781, ending the American War of Independence.

Even so, Comte de Vergennes was shocked at the concessions the British negotiators were willing to make, remarking to a friend that they gave up "all that I could have thought possible."[124] Historian Richard Morris agreed. Franklin and his team had had no real experience in such negotiating, but "were peers of their Old World counterparts at the finish."[125]

"Mon Chér Papa"

Even after the signing of the treaty Franklin remained in Paris for another two years as the American ambassador, meeting with European leaders to hammer out agreements between them and the infant American nation. "Treaties to be made with, I think, twenty powers in two years," he wrote to John Adams, "so that we are not likely to eat bread of idleness."[126]

With the stress of the war years behind him, Franklin was able to find time to relax in Paris. He enjoyed walking, although he had tended to slow down a bit with age. He found himself a fan of French cooking and loved his meals. As a result, he grew portly during the last few years in France and sometimes called himself "Dr. Fatsides."

In his years in France Franklin had thoroughly endeared himself to the French people and was very popular—especially with the ladies. He was known by many of them as *mon chér papa*, or "my darling father."

He wrote love poems to some of them and composed bawdy ballads, which he sang while accompanying himself on the harpsichord. There was much flirtation, and on at least one occasion Franklin proposed marriage.

The object of his affections was Mme. Helvetius, a sixty-year-old widow. She refused his offer of marriage, although she clearly adored Franklin. Their teasing and kissing in public—not uncommon in French society of the day—offended

Abigail Adams, who was in France while her husband John attended to political duties. Mrs. Adams was appalled at the way Mme. Helvetius's dressing gown came up higher than her feet when she sat down, and she wrote, "I was highly disgusted, and never wish for an acquaintance with ladies of this cast."[127]

The Final Voyage Home

Franklin was almost eighty when he received word from America that his mission was over. He was now in almost constant pain from a bladder stone and aching limbs. He said tearful goodbyes to friends in Passy and Paris. To one—an Englishman who had, along with Franklin, tried to find a compromise between the British and the Americans—he wrote his most tearful goodbye. He said that they had been fellow workers in the best of all jobs, the work of peace. "I leave you still in the field, but having finished my day's work, I am going home to go to bed! Wish me a good night's rest, as I do you a pleasant evening. Adieu!"[128]

Franklin was now "too feeble to walk or ride, [so] was taken out [to the ship] on one of the king's litters carried by mules."[129] Franklin carried with him a valuable gift from Louis XVI, a framed miniature portrait of the king, surrounded by 408 diamonds. (The portrait would be inherited by his daughter Sally, who would later sell it to finance her family's trip to Europe.)

Franklin's final voyage across the Atlantic was really no different from the many others he had made. He spent his time observing the waters of the Gulf

Franklin returns home from France to a hero's welcome. Nearly eighty years old, he hoped to retire from public life—but America was not finished with him yet.

Stream, writing letters, and even writing pamphlets on the importance of lifeboat drills and good diets for sailors!

When at last he reached Philadelphia Franklin was welcomed home with noise and crowds. Cannons boomed, and church bells rang throughout the city. The weary old man who needed help just to walk a few steps was a returned hero, and everyone wanted to say thank you.

He looked forward to going back to his home on Market Street to finish out the rest of his days quietly. Friends from the Continental Congress agreed that this was a good idea. But first, he was told, he had a few more tasks to perform.

Chapter

10 The Voice of Reason

Franklin hoped to put his public service career behind him when he returned to America. He looked forward to writing, reading, being with friends and family—and most of all—to pursuing his scientific interests. "I shall now be free of politics for the rest of my life," he wrote happily to a friend. "Welcome again, my dear philosophical amusements!"[130]

"I Find Myself Harnessed Again"

Upon returning to Philadelphia Franklin was nominated for a seat on the Pennsylvania Supreme Executive Council, the state's new legislative body. He won the election easily—without campaigning at all—and the following day was chosen the body's president.

Although a part of him must have been flattered, Franklin seemed disgusted in a letter he wrote in November 1785. "I find myself harnessed again in service for another year. They engrossed the prime of my life. They have eaten my flesh, and seem resolved now to pick my bones."[131]

Franklin served as the president of the Supreme Executive Council for a year. Even though he missed many meetings because of failing health, he was nominated at the end of that year's term to serve a second one. The election was not even close. The only vote against Franklin was his own.

Problems in the New Nation

By late 1786 there were problems in the new American nation. Having united long enough to win the war, the individual states were having difficulties getting along now that independence had finally been achieved. There were boundary disputes between states, which sometimes erupted into violence. Because each state printed its own paper money, they were often reluctant to accept one another's currency.

There was no strong central government, no force that could smooth the tensions that were building. The Articles of Confederation, an agreement outlining the new government of thirteen states written immediately after the war ended in 1781, was not working. Too much individual power had been granted to each state; it was like having thirteen separate nations trying to get along with one another.

"We discover some errors," wrote Franklin in 1786, "in our general and

The Pennsylvania statehouse where Franklin served as president of the Supreme Executive Council of the state for two years. Although he wanted only to retire to private life and enjoy his intellectual pursuits and his grandchildren, he did not refuse to serve when elected.

particular constitutions, which it is no wonder they should have, the time in which they were formed being considered. But these we shall mend." [132]

A Constitutional Convention

The way Franklin and his colleagues decided to mend the errors was to try to forge a better document than the Articles of Confederation. The Constitutional Convention met for the first time in Philadelphia in May 1787.

Of all the delegates to the convention, Franklin was the oldest. He was becoming increasingly frail, and even walking the few blocks to the meetings was impossible for him. Instead, he rode from his house to the convention meetings in a sort of "sultan's chair," carried by several inmates from the local prison.

He considered himself a delegate whose purpose was to listen, not to lead. He spoke far less than other delegates, content to throw in an occasional comment, or, when the mood was especially tense, a joke. Van Doren writes that Franklin was "a philosopher among them incomparably able, when he chose, to speak with large wisdom, the pleasantest humor, and a happy grace."[133]

Difficulty at the Convention

Franklin had definite ideas about how a federal government should be set up, but none of his ideas were agreed to. For instance, he favored a government with one legislature rather than two, and having multiple presidents, rather than one. He also firmly believed that no officer of the federal government should receive payment.

One of his ideas was accepted. Franklin surprised everyone late in the convention when he requested that the final sessions be opened with a prayer. He had never been a churchgoer and had always kept his beliefs to himself. Even so, he said, he did believe that God was evident in the events of people and that a divine presence would maybe help the states in their debates. A prayer might be a good

thing: "If a sparrow cannot fall to the ground without His notice," said Franklin, "is it probable that an empire can rise without His aid?"[134]

Even with the opening prayer the convention wore on in an endless chain of fights and squabbles. None of the delegates seemed to trust one another. The smaller states were convinced that they should get the same representation as large states in the new government, otherwise they would be swallowed up. The larger states objected, for they had more people and needed more representation. And neither small nor large states wanted to give too much power to a federal government, for then they would *all* be weaker.

Leaving Unified

At last, four months after it began, the Constitutional Convention had hammered out a plan for the organization of

A Most Extraordinary Man

During the proceedings of the 1787 Constitutional Convention, a delegate from Georgia, William Pierce, was impressed by Franklin's manner.

"It is certain that he [Franklin] does not shine much in public council; he is no speaker, nor does he seem to let politics engage his attention. He is, however, a most extraordinary man, and tells a story in a style more engaging than anything I ever heard. . . . He is 82 and possesses an activity of mind equal to a youth of 25 years of age."

(quoted in Van Doren, *Benjamin Franklin*)

the federal government. Most delegates were unhappy with it, for it was a compromise for nearly everyone. Each man in the convention felt his state had not been fairly treated or that the new plan was in some detail wrong.

On the day the Constitution was to be voted on and signed, Franklin asked for the floor. Stoop-shouldered and pale, he stood up and handed his written speech to fellow Pennsylvanian James Wilson, who read it to the delegates.

In the speech Franklin reminded the delegates that all people think they are infallible. He often did himself, and he knew the delegates did, too. But Franklin urged them to put aside their egos and their pride and think about the big picture.

The document might not be perfect, but it was as perfect as it could be, with so many different viewpoints included in it. The most important thing, he said, was to be united and unanimous in their support of the document so that their individual states would ratify it. The new nation could then get on with the business ahead.

"On the whole," wrote Franklin, "I cannot help expressing a wish that every member of the convention who may still have objections to it would, with me, on this occasion doubt a little of his own infallibility, and, to make manifest our unanimity, put his name to the instrument."[135]

The words had their desired effect. The Constitution was accepted and signed, and Franklin could finally go home.

The Final Days

Franklin lived two more years after the convention was over. He had his house on Market Street remodeled so that there would be plenty of space for his daughter Sally and her seven children to live there, too.

Nonpaying Jobs

Franklin believed strongly that high government positions should be nonpaying. In The Real Benjamin Franklin, *Andrew M. Allison quotes Franklin's address before the Constitutional Convention in 1787.*

"There are two passions which have a powerful influence in the affairs of men. These are *ambition* and *avarice;* the love of power and the love of money. Separately, each of these has great force in prompting men to action; but when united in view of the same object, they have in many minds the most violent effects. . . . [The type of people who would run for public office if it were profitable would not be] the wise and moderate, the lovers of peace and good order, the men fittest for the trust. It will be the bold and the violent, the men of strong passions and [tireless] activity in their selfish pursuits."

He kept up correspondence with old friends in America and Europe and read avidly. He was fascinated by the French Revolution, but horrified to learn that two of his good friends in France had died in the rebellion—one shot, the other executed at the guillotine.

Franklin's political interests had stayed keen, too. He took up the cause of abolition in his final years, believing that slavery was both immoral and impractical. Abolitionism was not a popular view in those days, even in northern states.

Franklin's grandchildren gave him pleasure, too. He did not leave his bedroom at all during the last year of his life and spent much of the time resting in bed. He kept a jar of sweet jelly on his nightstand, and when one of the small children drew him a picture or read to him, he would reward them with a spoonful of the jelly.

As his health deteriorated Franklin found the pain of his bladder stone excruciating. He was given opium as a painkiller, but it made him so drowsy and inattentive that he stopped taking it. At one point he seemed to rally, looking a little like his old self. His daughter remarked that maybe he would recover and live on a few more years. "I hope not," was Franklin's honest reply.[136]

He finally lapsed into a coma, and on April 17, 1790, Benjamin Franklin died.

"With Humorous Mastery"

Carl Van Doren writes that the moment a great person dies, another story begins—that of "his continuing influence, his changing renown, the legend which takes the place of fact."[137]

This French engraving of Franklin captures his engaging presence and relaxed manner.

Franklin's genius needs no exaggeration. But a list of accomplishments and public achievements cannot possibly be equated to the value of Benjamin Franklin's life. He was more than the visible contributions he left behind. Franklin provided Americans with an image, a man at home among royalty and common people alike, and beloved by both. He excelled both in public domains like diplomacy and politics, and in the intensely isolated disciplines of science and writing. A statesman, a politician, an inventor, a writer, a scientist, a public servant, a diplomat—in a world that would have respected him for excelling as any of these, he excelled as all of them.

Regards from General Washington

A few days before his death Franklin received a letter from his good friend George Washington, who wished him relief from his constant pain. This excerpt is from Frank Donovan's book, The Benjamin Franklin Papers.

"Would to God, my dear sir, that I could congratulate you upon the removal of that excruciating pain under which you labor, and that your existence might close with as much ease to yourself as its continuance has been beneficial to our country and useful to mankind; or, if the united wishes of a free people, joined with the earnest prayers of every friend to science and humanity, could relieve the body from pain or infirmities, that you could claim an exemption on this score. But this cannot be, and you have within yourself the only resource to which we can confidently apply for relief, a philosophic mind."

George Washington, like so many others, revered and admired Benjamin Franklin.

But what about Franklin's relevance today? How is our modern age different because of his life? Without him, say historians, the alliance with France that contributed to American independence would have been doubtful. And without the alliance guaranteeing French support, the Continental army quite probably would have been defeated.

The scientific discoveries and inventions, too, were Franklin's legacy to the future; many of his observations and inventions are as useful today as they were in the eighteenth century.

There are other ways in which Franklin's significance is felt in modern times. Historian Esmond Wright believes that Franklin would have been more at home today than in his own time. Franklin was rational and pragmatic. Says Wright, Franklin

> did not like obscurities or words from the clouds. He required that the universe be capable of comprehension. . . . Man for [Franklin] was an animal who made tools, built stoves, and cured smoky chimneys. He worked in the light. . . . This was a cool man, a man the twentieth century can appreciate even more than did the eighteenth.[138]

Franklin was different from so many others of his day, not just in his intelligence and talent, but because he could attend to political details while keeping the "big picture" in sight. He was a global man, as Wright points out, "far in advance of his time, not merely as editor turned scientist turned statesman . . . but because one is aware of his own awareness of challenges and of the immense potential of the human mind when left free to speculate, to question, and to experiment."[139]

Franklin envisioned a time when the world had no artificial boundaries and there was no abridgement of freedom or basic rights. In one of his last letters Franklin wrote to David Hartley, a friend from England: "God grant that not only the love of liberty but a thorough knowledge of the rights of man may pervade all the nations of the earth so that a philosopher may set his foot anywhere on its surface and say, 'This is my country.'"[140]

A Personal Tang

The years of Franklin's time were rich with creative and innovative personalities. Just within his circle of acquaintances in America there were many people whose names are well known as patriots and strong leaders, such as George Washington, Thomas Jefferson, and John Adams. Yet because of his style Franklin stands alone.

He was more than a generation older than the other founding fathers, but it has been said that of all of them, Franklin is the only one whose name elicits a smile. He had what Van Doren calls a "personal tang," a spirit of constant optimism and humor that set the rules he lived by. Such a spirit allowed Franklin to move through his many worlds with grace.

Notes

Introduction: A Harmonious Human Multitude

1. Carl Van Doren, *Benjamin Franklin,* New York: Viking Press, 1938.

2. Van Doren, *Benjamin Franklin.*

3. Esmond Wright, *Franklin of Philadelphia.* Cambridge, MA: Harvard University Press, 1986.

4. Letter from Franklin to Jane Mecom, October 25, 1779, quoted in Van Doren, *Benjamin Franklin.*

5. Van Doren, *Benjamin Franklin.*

6. Van Doren, *Benjamin Franklin.*

7. Quoted in Van Doren, *Benjamin Franklin.*

8. Mark Twain, "The Late Benjamin Franklin," reprinted in *The Saturday Evening Post,* March 1983.

Chapter 1: A Boston Boyhood

9. Benjamin Franklin, *Autobiography.*

10. Franklin, *Autobiography.*

11. Franklin, *Autobiography.*

12. Franklin, *Autobiography.*

13. Franklin, *Autobiography.*

14. Ronald W. Clark, *Benjamin Franklin.* New York: Random House, 1983.

15. Clark, *Benjamin Franklin.*

16. Franklin, *Autobiography.*

17. Franklin, *Autobiography.*

18. Franklin, *Autobiography.*

19. Van Doren, *Benjamin Franklin.*

20. Franklin, *Autobiography.*

21. Franklin, *Autobiography.*

22. Franklin, *Autobiography.*

23. Franklin, *Autobiography.*

24. Franklin, *Autobiography.*

25. Franklin, *Autobiography.*

26. Franklin, *Autobiography.*

Chapter 2: A Rising Star

27. Franklin, *Autobiography.*

28. Franklin, *Autobiography.*

29. Franklin, *Autobiography.*

30. Franklin, *Autobiography.*

31. Franklin, *Autobiography.*

32. Franklin, *Autobiography.*

33. Franklin, *Autobiography.*

34. Franklin, *Autobiography.*

35. Milton Meltzer, *Benjamin Franklin: The New American.* New York: Franklin Watts, 1988.

Chapter 3: A New Leaf

36. Clark, *Benjamin Franklin.*

37. Clark, *Benjamin Franklin.*

38. Clark, *Benjamin Franklin.*

39. Thomas Fleming, *The Man Who Dared Lightning.* New York: William Morrow, 1971.

40. Clark, *Benjamin Franklin.*

41. Clark, *Benjamin Franklin.*

42. Franklin, *Autobiography.*

43. Catherine Drinker Bowen, *The Most Dangerous Man in America.* Boston: Little, Brown, 1974.

44. Quoted in Bowen, *The Most Dangerous Man in America*.

45. Van Doren, *Benjamin Franklin*.

46. Van Doren, *Benjamin Franklin*.

47. Franklin, *Autobiography*.

48. Franklin, *Autobiography*.

49. (from *Poor Richard's Almanack)*, quoted in Wright, *Franklin of Philadelphia*.

Chapter 4: From Private Citizen to Public Figure

50. Franklin, *Autobiography*.

51. Wright, *Franklin of Philadelphia*.

52. Bowen, *The Most Dangerous Man in America*.

53. Franklin, *Autobiography*.

54. Franklin, *Autobiography*.

55. Van Doren, *Benjamin Franklin*.

56. Franklin, *Autobiography*.

57. Van Doren, *Benjamin Franklin*.

58. Wright, *Franklin of Philadelphia*.

59. Franklin, *Autobiography*.

Chapter 5: The Scientist and Inventor

60. Van Doren, *Benjamin Franklin*.

61. Van Doren, *Benjamin Franklin*.

62. Letter to Peter Collinson, quoted in Meltzer, *Benjamin Franklin: The New American*.

63. Frank Donovan, *The Benjamin Franklin Papers*. New York: Dodd, Mead, and Co., 1962.

64. Clark, *Benjamin Franklin*.

65. Bowen, *The Most Dangerous Man in America*.

66. Thomas Fleming, *Benjamin Franklin*. New York: Four Winds Press, 1972.

67. Benjamin Franklin, *Experiments and Observations on Electricity*. July 1750, quoted in Meltzer, *Benjamin Franklin: The New American*.

68. Van Doren, *Benjamin Franklin*.

69. Quoted in Clark, *Benjamin Franklin*.

70. Quoted in Clark, *Benjamin Franklin*.

71. Van Doren, *Benjamin Franklin*.

72. Van Doren, *Benjamin Franklin*.

73. Wright, *Franklin of Philadelphia*.

Chapter 6: Thinking Continentally

74. Bowen, *The Most Dangerous Man in America*.

75. Van Doren, *Benjamin Franklin*.

76. Bowen, *The Most Dangerous Man in America*.

77. *The Pennsylvania Gazette*, May 9, 1751, quoted in Andrew M. Allison, ed., *The Real Benjamin Franklin*. Salt Lake City: The Freeman Institute, 1982.

78. Bowen, *The Most Dangerous Man in America*.

79. Quoted in Allison, *The Real Benjamin Franklin*.

80. Van Doren, *Benjamin Franklin*.

81. Letter to Deborah Franklin, January 25, 1756, quoted in Van Doren, *Benjamin Franklin*.

Chapter 7: Making Enemies

82. Van Doren, *Benjamin Franklin*.

83. Letter to Richard Peters, May 14, 1757, quoted in Van Doren, *Benjamin Franklin*.

84. Letter to Mary Stevenson, March 25, 1763, quoted in Allison, *The Real Benjamin Franklin*.

85. Willard Randall, *A Little Revenge: Benjamin Franklin and His Son*. Boston: Little, Brown, 1984.

86. Letter to Deborah Franklin, February 19, 1758, quoted in Van Doren, *Benjamin Franklin*.

87. Benjamin Franklin, *A Narrative of the Late Massacres in Lancaster County*, January 1764, quoted in John Updike, "Many Bens," *New Yorker*, February 22, 1988.

88. Letter to Lord Kames, June 2, 1765, quoted in Clark, *Benjamin Franklin*.

89. Fleming, *Benjamin Franklin*.

90. Letter to John Hughes, August 9, 1765, quoted in Van Doren, *Benjamin Franklin*.

91. Letter to Deborah Franklin, November 9, 1765, quoted in Van Doren, *Benjamin Franklin*.

92. Van Doren, *Benjamin Franklin*.

Chapter 8: Moving Toward War

93. Quoted in Van Doren, *Benjamin Franklin*.

94. Letter to William Franklin, March 13, 1768, quoted in Van Doren, *Benjamin Franklin*.

95. Letter to William Franklin, October 6, 1773, quoted in Wright, *Franklin of Philadelphia*.

96. Letter to Jane Mecom, November 1, 1773, quoted in Van Doren, *Benjamin Franklin*.

97. Alice Hall, "Philosopher of Dissent: Benjamin Franklin," *National Geographic*, July 1975.

98. Hall, *National Geographic*, July 1975.

99. Letter to Thomas Cushing, February 2, 1774, quoted in Van Doren, *Benjamin Franklin*.

100. Bowen, *The Most Dangerous Man in America*.

101. Bowen, *The Most Dangerous Man in America*.

102. Donovan, *The Benjamin Franklin Papers*.

103. Letter to William Franklin, March 22, 1775.

104. Letter to Thomas Cushing, February 15, 1774.

105. Letter to Deborah Franklin, April 28, 1774.

106. Van Doren, *Benjamin Franklin*.

107. Frank Donovan, *The Many Worlds of Benjamin Franklin*. Mahwah, NJ: Troll Associates, 1963.

108. Donovan, *The Many Worlds of Benjamin Franklin*.

109. Wright, *Franklin of Philadelphia*.

110. Wright, *Franklin of Philadelphia*.

Chapter 9: The Diplomat in Paris

111. Wright, *Franklin of Philadelphia*.

112. Van Doren, *Benjamin Franklin*.

113. Letter to Mrs. Thompson, February 8, 1777, quoted in Van Doren, *Benjamin Franklin*.

114. Letter to Thomas Digges, June 25, 1780, quoted in Van Doren, *Benjamin Franklin*.

115. Fleming, *The Man Who Dared the Lightning*.

116. Van Doren, *Benjamin Franklin*.

117. Letter to John Jay, October 2, 1780, quoted in Van Doren, *Benjamin Franklin*.

118. Van Doren, *Benjamin Franklin*.

119. Letter to Arthur Lee, April 3, 1778, quoted in Van Doren, *Benjamin Franklin*.

120. Van Doren, *Benjamin Franklin.*

121. *New Jersey Gazette,* October 2, 1777, quoted in Wright, *Franklin of Philadelphia.*

122. Letter to John Adams, October 2, 1780, quoted in Van Doren, *Benjamin Franklin.*

123. Van Doren, *Benjamin Franklin.*

124. Van Doren, *Benjamin Franklin.*

125. Richard Morris, *The Peacemakers and American Independence.* New York: Harper & Row, 1965.

126. Wright, *Franklin of Philadelphia.*

127. Quoted in Wright, *Franklin of Philadelphia.*

128. Wright, *Franklin of Philadelphia.*

129. Meltzer, *Benjamin Franklin: The New American.*

Chapter 10: The Voice of Reason

130. Letter to Jan Ingenhousz, April 24, 1785, quoted in Wright, *Franklin of Philadelphia.*

131. Letter to Dr. and Mrs. John Bard, November 14, 1785, quoted in Van Doren, *Benjamin Franklin.*

132. Letter to Edward Bancroft, November 26, 1786, quoted in Van Doren, *Benjamin Franklin.*

133. Van Doren, *Benjamin Franklin.*

134. Van Doren, *Benjamin Franklin.*

135. Van Doren, *Benjamin Franklin.*

136. Van Doren, *Benjamin Franklin.*

137. Van Doren, *Benjamin Franklin.*

138. Wright, *Franklin of Philadelphia.*

139. Wright, *Franklin of Philadelphia.*

140. Meltzer, *Benjamin Franklin: The New American.*

For Further Reading

Andrew M. Allison, ed., *The Real Benjamin Franklin*. Salt Lake City: The Freeman Institute, 1982.

James C. Baughman, "Sense Is Preferable to Sound," *Library Journal*, October 15, 1986.

Frederic A. Birmingham, "The Infinite Riches of Ben Franklin," *The Saturday Evening Post*, March 1982.

Frank Donovan, *The Benjamin Franklin Papers*. New York: Dodd, Mead, and Co., 1962.

Frank Donovan, *The Many Worlds of Benjamin Franklin*. Mahwah, NJ: Troll Associates, 1963.

Thomas Fleming, *Benjamin Franklin*. New York: Four Winds Press, 1972.

Benjamin Franklin, *Autobiography* (many editions available).

Benjamin Franklin, "The Rattle Snake as a Symbol of America," reprinted from *Pennsylvania Journal*, December 27, 1775, in *American Heritage*, March 1988.

Claude-Ann Lopez and Eugenia W. Herbert, *The Private Franklin: The Man and His Family*. New York: W. W. Norton, 1975.

Milton Meltzer, *Benjamin Franklin: The New American*. New York: Franklin Watts, 1988.

Mark Twain, "The Late Benjamin Franklin," reprinted in *The Saturday Evening Post*, March 1983.

Works Consulted

Peter Baida, "Mr. Franklin's Leadership Maxims," *American Hertitage*, August 1986. An informative article setting Franklin's ideas on business and leadership in a modern context.

Catherine Drinker Bowen, *The Most Dangerous Man in America*. Boston: Little, Brown, 1974. A readable account of Franklin's adult life, with particular emphasis on his pre-war contributions.

Ronald W. Clark, *Benjamin Franklin*. New York: Random House, 1983. An interesting biography, with excellent notes and bibliography.

Thomas Fleming, *The Man Who Dared the Lightning*. New York: William Morrow, 1971. An entertaining account of Franklin's adult life.

Alice Hall, "Philosopher of Dissent: Benjamin Franklin," *National Geographic*, July 1975. Helpful article about the Philadelphia "stomping grounds" of Franklin, with excellent accompanying photographs.

Edmund S. Morgan, "Secrets of Benjamin Franklin," *New York Review of Books*, January 31, 1991. Interesting article addressing Franklin's effects—both positive and negative—on his times.

Richard B. Morris, *The Peacemakers and American Independence*. New York: Harper & Row, 1965. Very readable with an excellent bibliography.

Willard Randall, *A Little Revenge: Benjamin Franklin and His Son*. Boston: Little, Brown, 1984. Though difficult reading, the author offers fascinating glimpses into the complex relationship between Franklin and his son.

Ormond Seavey, *Becoming Benjamin Franklin: The Autobiography and the Life*. University Park: Pennsylvania State University Press, 1988. Helpful notes and bibliography, though very difficult reading.

Charles Tanford, *Ben Franklin Stilled the Waves*. Durham, NC: Duke University Press, 1989. A fascinating account of Franklin's various scientific pursuits.

John Updike, "Many Bens," *New Yorker*, February 22, 1988. A very entertaining account of the many facets of Franklin, addressing how he has been misunderstood by many.

Carl Van Doren, *Benjamin Franklin*. New York: Viking Press, 1938. The definitive biography of Franklin, with extensive quotations and sources.

Esmond Wright, *Franklin of Philadelphia*. Cambridge, MA: Harvard University Press, 1986. A good biography, with an extensive bibliography.

P. M. Zell, *Franklin's Autobiography: A Model Life*. Boston: Twayne Publishing, 1989. A companion piece to Franklin's *Autobiography*. Helpful editing puts Franklin's words into historical context.

Index

Picture Credits

Cover photo by Library of Congress

AIP Niels Bohr Library, 33

American Philosophical Society, 39 (right), 41, 57 (both)

The Bettmann Archive, 11, 19, 22, 24, 29 (bottom), 45, 46, 47 (left), 56, 64, 65 (bottom),74, 75, 95, 104

Courtesy CIGNA Museum and Art Collection, 27, 42, 50

Historical Pictures/Stock Montage, 14, 32, 36, 38, 47 (right), 68 (both), 70, 72, 77

Historical Society of Pennsylvania, 29 (top), 76

Library of Congress, 10, 13, 15, 21, 23, 28, 37, 43, 49, 58, 61, 63, 65 (top), 66, 80, 81, 82, 88 (both), 90, 91, 93 (top left, bottom), 96, 98 (both), 100, 103 (both), 109, 110

Library Company of Philadelphia, 39 (left)

National Archives, 7, 86, 93 (middle), 101

About the Author

Gail B. Stewart received her undergraduate degree from Gustavus Adolphus College in St. Peter, Minnesota. She did her graduate work in English, linguistics, and curriculum study at the College of St. Thomas and the University of Minnesota. Stewart taught English and reading for more than ten years.

She has written over forty-eight books for young people, including a six-part series called *Living Spaces*. She has written several books for Lucent Books including *Drug Trafficking* and *Acid Rain*.

Stewart and her husband live in Minneapolis with their three sons, two dogs, and a cat. She enjoys reading (especially children's books) and playing tennis.